THE DEEP SPACE LOG BOOK
A FIRST SEASON COMPANION

By Mark A. Altman and Edward Gross

BOXTREE

First published in the UK 1994
by BOXTREE LIMITED, Broadwall House
21 Broadwall, London SE1 9PL

First published in the USA 1993 by Image Publishing

10 9 8 7 6 5 4 3 2 1

Copyright © 1994 Edward Gross and Mark A. Altman

Cover Photo: Commander Benjamin Sisko and
Captain Jean Luc Picard (photo copyright © 1994
David Strick/Onyx)
Back cover: A gather of the ''Deep Space'' ensemble
(photo copyright © 1994 Celebrity Photo Agency)
Photo page 4: copyright © 1994 Gamma Liaison
Some photographs courtesy Karen Witkowski

ISBN: 1 85283 388 2

Printed and bound in Finland by Werner Söderström Oy

TABLE OF CONTENTS

Introduction 5

Chapter One: The Golden Child..7

Chapter Two: Rick Berman 13

Chapter Three: Michael Piller...16

Chapter Four: Welcome to Bajor 18

Chapter Five: Singing The Sound Stage Blues 21

Chapter Six: As The Space Station Turns 31

Chapter Seven: Get Thee To The Gamma Quadrant 42

Season One Episode Guide...47

    "Emissary" 49

    "Past Prologue" 55

    "A Man Alone" 56

    "Babel" 59

    "Captive Pursuit" 60

    "Q-Less" 61

    "Dax" 65

    "The Passenger" 67

    "Move Along Home" 69

    "The Nagus" 71

    "Vortex" 73

    "Battle Lines" 75

    "The Storyteller" 77

    "Progess" 78

    "If Wishes Were Horses" 80

    "The Forsaken" 82

    "Dramatis Personae" 84

    "Duet" 85

    "In the Hands of the Prophets" 87

Appendix A: The Comic..90

Appendix B: The Next Generation On Deep Space.................94

Appendix C: A Day In The Life 96

Appendix D: Question & Answer Session 100

The criticism voiced by fans after the premiere of DEEP SPACE NINE's two-hour opener, "Emissary", evoked a strange sense of deja vu. It had only been five years before that "Encounter At Farpoint" had unspooled on televisions across America and many rabid Trek-philes had denounced the series for straying too far from the established Trekkian lore. Quick to condemn the show as the height of sacrilege, those same fans are now ardent followers of NEXT GENERATION.

The reaction to DEEP SPACE NINE has been similar. The series is an even more dramatic departure from the original show than THE NEXT GENERATION was. Despite its STAR TREK credentials, DS9 — as the series has become known — was created after the death of Gene Roddenberry and rather than take place on a starship, is set on a space station. Along with its grittier venue and darker themes, DS9 has proven a mixed bag to many viewers.

To us, DS9 is a triumph. Its creators, Rick Berman and Michael Piller,, rather than feel constrained by the limitations of the franchise, chose to expand the envelope of the TREK universe. In a town, Hollywood, where commerciality is king and retreads and remakes abound, Piller, Berman and Paramount had the vision to truly boldly go where TREK had never gone before. It would have been easy to set the sequel series on another starship with the familiar Starfleet trappings, but instead DS9 is an engrossing concoction of tried and true TREK philosophy with a '90s spin. DS9 is truly a product of its time. In the same way that the racial strife and battle lines over the Vietnam conflict shaped the philosophy of the original STAR TREK and the sense of '80s optimism and consensus building leadership style of George Bush defined the late '80s and early part of this decade, DS9's more tentative, problem-plagued view of the future reflects the divided international landscape of the '90s as we head into the new millennia.

As Michael Piller pointed out, "Emissary's" teleplay and tone was affected dramatically by the 1992 Los Angeles Riots. Ironically, the producers almost seemed prescient in the way that their fictional Bajoran/Cardassian conflict predated the war in Bosnia and the disintegration of Yugoslovia. Even more remarkable was the coincidence of the series' three-part second season opener with a failed attempt by hardliners in Russia to unseat populist President Boris Yeltsin mirroring the chaos on Bajor.

Some fans prefer the unblemished optimism of previous TREKs, free of the challenging philosophies and fatalistic moments of despair that typify the new series. We do not. To us, DS9 represents television at its best: compelling characters, thoughtful storytelling, a socio-political awareness and a strong ensemble of actors combined with entertaining adventures. DS9 in its first season was far from always successful. It was uneven and flawed as it struggled to define itself, but that is to be expected. The NEXT GENERATION experienced the same growing pains in its infancy moving on from shows like "Home Soil" to sixth season's "Tapestry". However, if DS9's final episodes are any indication of the promise of the series' future, the new TREK will apparently offer a wealth of entertainment, awe and contemplation; the essential ingredients which have sustained STAR TREK for three decades and will continue to stoke the warp engines of all of the Paramount's TREKs to come.. We look forward to sharing in the adventures.

Welcome aboard.

Mark A. Altman
Edward Gross

December 1993

Jan. 2-8

TV GUIDE

®

89¢

STAR TREK'S
NEWEST FRONTIER
DEEP SPACE NINE

Bill Bixby
fights for his life

**Long Island
Lolita**
One crime,
three TV movies

Charles & Di
Sneak peek
at <u>the</u> movie

01

EXCLUSIVE PHOTOS

1ST EPISODE
PLOT SECRETS

SPECIAL TO TVG:
CAPT. PICARD
BRIDGES THE <u>NEXT</u>
GENERATION GAP

Avery

6

CHAPTER ONE

THE GOLDEN CHILD

DEEP SPACE NINE in its first year drew consistently strong ratings, eventually settling in a few ratings points behind it sister series, THE NEXT GENERATION — itself a ratings juggernaut whose numbers continued to improve throughout its sixth season. While there has been some erosion in DEEP SPACE's ratings since its record-shattering premiere, the show remained second only to THE NEXT GENERATION in the syndicated one-hour dramatic category ratings.

"I'm very pleased with the way the first season has gone in a lot of respects," said Executive Producer and Co-Creator Rick Berman. "First seasons of television shows tend to be potentially very chaotic. The first season of NEXT GENERATION certainly was. This season has been very peaceful in terms of the actors, the crew, the writers and the budgets. As far as the episodes, there are things about them that I love and things about them I don't love. That's the way it is, if we were completely satisfied with what we did, we wouldn't be doing what we do. We're always looking to make things better. What I'm most pleased with is the fact that the concept is working and we've managed to create 20 stories that I think all hang pretty well on the armature that we've built, the backstory and the characters."

Ironically, for a show rife with a myriad of logistical problems during its launch, the start-up was devoid of long-lasting strife. "I think basically what we had was money from Paramount, the support of Paramount and we've been left alone by Paramount," stated Supervising Producer Ira Steven Behr, who returned to STAR TREK after having served as a writer/producer during THE NEXT GENERATION's third year. "We were trying to create episodes for the series without even having a pilot shot, which was very difficult. This was a show that was treated with kid gloves and given every chance in the world to make good. We were able to reshoot scenes in the pilot that didn't work, money was given, we could tinker with the sets when we didn't like the way they looked. Being part of the STAR TREK phenomenon has really helped because this wasn't a show where the studio saw a possible thirteen episodes with a pickup for a season, and then maybe it'll get two or three years. They saw this as continuing the franchise, so the start-up was not difficult on that level."

"I thought it was going to be much tougher," said Siddig El Fadil, who was discovered in England for the part of Dr. Julian Bashir. "The last thing I was doing was working in Israel on the West Bank on the Gaza Strip with fake Israeli soldiers and real Muslim Palestinians around. That was tough and very hard work. There were grueling sand storms every day — so compared to that, this has been fine. I've been lucky, I've been working fairly regularly so I've had a nice chunk of every show and it's been easy to pace myself. I haven't had too heavy a social life to deal with."

Unlike "Encounter At Farpoint," where the studio was dubious of the fledgling NEXT GENERATION's potential, fearing that audiences would not embrace a new cast of characters and actors, DEEP SPACE NINE has had the benefit of NEXT GENERATION's groundbreaking success, proving that a sequel series could become a greater ratings and, arguably, aesthetic triumph than the show which spawned it.

"I was on the pilot of THE NEXT GENERATION so I knew what this was going to be like," said Supervising Producer David Livingston, who oversees the physical production of the show for Rick Berman. "One of the reservations II had about working on the show this year was because I knew how hard it is to do a pilot and how challenging it would be. But since I had gone through it once, I knew what to be prepared for. And, you know, they made me an offer II couldn't refuse. So I did it and I'm thrilled I did it. I wouldn't want to be anywhere else."

"I'm very proud of it," said Co-Creator and Executive Producer Michael Piller of DEEP SPACE's freshman year in space. "It's a really good television show. It might not be the cup of tea for everyone and maybe it turns off some NEXT GENERATION fans because it has a little rougher edge around it, but I had a wonderful time doing it. It has not been a brutal season, it has been enjoyable working with Ira Behr, who is funny and talented and I am so lucky to have lured him back here. [Co-Producer] Peter Fields is one of the great characters in Hollywood that I have encountered, he has millions of story, he'll tell you stories about actors and stars and every time we sit down at a table and start talking about something totally irrelevant, he'll say, 'Oh yeah, I was on a plane with Jane Fonda, she got me arrested as a matter of fact.'"

Before DEEP SPACE NINE's premiere, there was some concern that the premise of the show — which is set on a space station adjacent to the galaxy's first stable wormhole — would prove too constraining. Many have attributed STAR TREK's long term success to the Enterprise itself, pointing out that the ship has been the true star of the show. Berman and Piller, however, have proven that one does not need a starship to continue charting the STAR TREK universe.

Said Berman, "It's very frustrating sometimes not having the Enterprise to be able to take you to warp six and places unknown, but I think considering what we have constructed and the situation with Bajor and the space station, the writing staff and the actors and everyone involved is starting to become more acclimated to it and I think it's just going to continue to get better. If you go back to look at some of the episodes of the first season of THE NEXT GENERATION, you'll see actors who weren't all that familiar with their characters and characters who weren't familiar with their relationships with other characters. These things grow."

"Good drama is good

drama," said Co-Producer Peter Allan Fields, who left the staff of NEXT GENERATION to join DEEP SPACE NINE. "The thing that scared me at first was when they told me it's about a space station next to a wormhole. First, I didn't know what a wormhole was. Secondly, the Enterprise's mission was to boldly go where no one has gone before and from what Michael told me about DS9, we were going to boldly sit where no one had sat before. I didn't really get a laugh when I said it, because I was serious, but it's actually been just fine."

Fields pointed out that he sees STAR TREK less as a science-fiction show than a period piece, simply set in the future instead of the past. "One of the things that detracts from DEEP SPACE NINE in the eyes of some snobs is you see people in alien masks and garb that we conceived for 24th century people and it looks like a costume parody to them," he said. "That sometimes does an injustice to the very real drama of things. There have been shows that had they been done in a suit and tie, assuming they could have been, would have been Emmy winners. If it's about people and emotions, which includes aliens, then you've got drama. It doesn't mean melodrama — and it can include comedic moments. What Gene Roddenberry wanted to do was to create a 24th century for which we could all work towards and look forward to and I think he's done that. I don't think it matters whether you're writing it about guys in tight pants in Sherwood Forest or the Death Star somewhere.

It's just good drama."

The key to creating DEEP SPACE NINE's "good drama" has been devising compelling characters which included casting talented actors who took the show's premise seriously. It's an evolution that has continued throughout the year. "You create characters and you continue to give words to those characters, but the actors who you hire bring an element to those characters," said Rick Berman. "The element that they bring week after week causes you to write slightly differently, and slowly, over the course of several years, the characters start developing in a much fuller and richer way. The actors start to get to know the characters better and they get to know what their relationship with the other characters are. The writers see this and feel it and it's a real collective effort on our part and the part of the actors in bringing these characters to life, making them more complex and giving them new layers. I've been delighted to see that that's happened in a very positive sense with everyone of our characters on the show."

"We were a mid-season show that started gearing up about a decade before we had to start shooting," commented Ira Behr about the considerable amount of prep time the series was given by the studio both on a creative and production level. "We had that luxury and I think that helped. A number of characters changed. I think Bashir changed, Dax changed, Sisko changed, Odo changed in terms of what Michael and I had basically

"Deep Space Nine" is the first "Star Trek" series to be produced without the guidance of Gene Roddenberry, though both Michael Piller and Rick Berman feel as though he has been on their shoulders the entire time (photo copyright © 1994 Karen Witkowski)

talked about in the very, very beginning. We finally had to say this going to be a little different than we anticipated, how do we make it work?"

Ultimately, the most important aspect of the new series for the producers was making the show less constraining in terms of allowing interpersonal conflict between the characters. "The problem with STAR TREK: THE NEXT GENERATION is Gene created a group of characters that he purposely chose not to allow conflict between," said Berman. "Starfleet officers cannot be in conflict and thus it's murderous to write these shows because there is no good drama without conflict and the conflict has to come from outside the group."

In order to bring conflict to the 24th century without violating the Roddenberry dictum governing his universe, Berman and Piller agreed to introduce non-Starfleet personnel into the mix who aren't governed by the same set of constraints that Federation officers had been in the previous series. "We set out to do something that was somewhat paradoxical, which was to bring conflict but not to break away from Gene's rules," said Berman. "They still play paramount importance in what we're doing and we created an environment where Starfleet officers were in a location that they weren't happy about being in and they were in a location where the people who lived there weren't all that happy about them being there. We also created a situation where people who were members of our core group were

not Starfleet: the security shape shifter Odo, the Bajoran major Kira, the bartender Quark. A group of our integral people are not Starfleet officers and the ones that are Starfleet officers aren't crazy about where they are, so we have a lot of frustration and conflict."

Michael Piller disagreed that the emphasis on Bajoran spirituality and secular beliefs goes against the atheist, antireligious beliefs of Roddenberry.

"I don't think it goes against Gene," he said. "If he was still with us — and he's still on our shoulders as we think about these conceptual issues — I don't think it would bother him one bit. What he felt very strongly about is that humans, and to some degree Federation members, had a humanist attitude; logic and reality. His humans do not overtly celebrate religious beliefs. What we have simply done in creating an environment that will bring conflict to our people, which we wanted to desperately do, was to put a group of people with a group of aliens that are different than we are, who had a conflict with our humanist beliefs. By giving them strong spiritual mystical orb and prophet worship, it forces our humanist people to deal with another alien race that is as different form us as the Klingons are. But they're different in the spirituality of their existence. We're saying if there's a problem here, let's fix the problem and they're saying the prophets have to be satisfied and that causes conflict. Gene would be the first to tell you it doesn't matter what alien race you're talking about, how hideous they seem to be, that

there are no bad aliens. Each of them have a culture within itself which must be defined and recognized and appreciated for what it is. We're simply creating a new alien race with a new set of circumstances and not changing Gene's vision of what humanity is in the 24th century, and we're simply showing how we are affected by that conflict with that alien race."

"I think Piller and Rick are both in a very good place," said DEEP SPACE writer/producer Ira Steven Behr. "With all the hassles of doing two shows and mistakes and all the things that happen, we all get along and it's been fun. I kept saying to Mike and Rick I don't want to go back and do STAR TREK again and, good or bad, they kept saying, 'We're really trying to keep it in the whole STAR TREK ethos, but we're going to make this a different show.' and I'm thinking this is easy to say, but once you've done something it's tough to suddenly shift gears and do this other thing and do them both at the same time. I was a bit skeptical and then I read the pilot, and I started to say 'Hmm, this has some potential.' What I was figuring was if you're going to have two hours of STAR TREK on a week, not counting all the repeats, they really have to be different than each other. People are getting their orgasm off watching THE NEXT GENERATION; once a week is enough for most people. We're asking them to come again and in order to do that you have to give them different stuff and I think that's what we're doing. As I sat there and watched dailies, I kept saying to Rick and

Michael, people are going to be surprised about this show.

"Not that it's this angst ridden, existential show," he continued. "I'm not trying to make it more than it is. It's still an hour of television, it's still an hour of STAR TREK television. But there's definite conflict and there are characters who are carrying all kinds of things around with them. I'm not just talking about Sisko losing his wife — which is a nice television convention — but there's people like Odo and Kira who are intensely driven people with things they have to deal with, and you wind up watching a lot of scenes where people are not agreeing with each other. Also, the look of the show has a feeling that's a lot different in the lighting and the architecture than THE NEXT GENERATION."

The cover of Pocket Books' first original "Deep Space Nine" novel, "The Siege"

#91, May/June '93

$2.50-U.S.

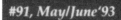

STAR TREK
THE OFFICIAL FAN CLUB

EXCLUSIVE INTERVIEW

RICK BERMAN

BEHIND-THE-SCENES ON
DEEP SPACE NINE
AND THE NEW
STAR TREK: THE NEXT GENERATION
FEATURE FILM!

This issue of "The Official Star Trek Fan Club" magazine features executive producer Rick Berman flanked by Commander Sisko (Avery Brooks) and Captain Picard (Patrick Stewart)

CHAPTER TWO

RICK BERMAN: GREAT BIRD OF THE GAMMA QUADRANT

When such power brokers as Michael Milken and Ivan Boesky were referred to as "masters of the universe," it wasn't necessarily an appellation of affection. In the case of Executive Producer Rick Berman, master of the TREK universe, it is a moniker that signifies his importance in having become the reigning benevolent monarch of Paramount's TREK empire, having long ago replaced Gene Roddenberry as the creative force behind the production and creative development of the STAR TREK franchise.

While Roddenberry's vision for the show continues to serve as the conceptual template which shapes the underlying philosophy of both TREK shows, it is Rick Berman who has been most responsible for the success of TREK in the 90's and transplanting the idealism of Roddenberry and Gene L. Coon into a palatable formula for jaded '90s television viewers.

Berman has overseen the production of STAR TREK: THE NEXT GENERATION for the last six years and more recently co-created DEEP SPACE NINE with Michael Piller. He is now shepherding the NEXT GENERATION movie to the screen as its Executive Producer as well and is developing STAR TREK: VOYAGER, the new series to debut in January '95.

Despite his intimate involvement in all things TREK, Berman continues to immerse himself in the day-to-day production of both series, although the increased workload has forced him to scale back his involvement. "My involvement in every element in the THE NEXT GENERATION; the stories, the drafts of the script, the design work, the visuals, the casting, the production elements, the music spotting, the sound, the editing, the dubbing, was very, very intense. With DEEP SPACE NINE coming along I couldn't do that double, so I had to step back a little bit and let other people do some of it. That was the most difficult thing for me. Much more difficult than doing more work was doing less work, but I have come to a relatively good balance. I would say I do half the work I used to do on NEXT GENERATION. On DEEP SPACE NINE I do 3/4 of what I used to do on NEXT GENERATION. That means I'm putting in 70 hours as opposed to 55, but I've managed to do that at the price of not being as much in control and as much on the pulse of what's going on with either one. Seventy-five percent on my time is DEEP SPACE NINE and 50% on NEXT GENERATION. The movies are taking up more of my time now. When we're producing the movies, it'll be done during the hiatus so that will be feasible and my involvement with the post-production on the movie will not be that major. It's spread out over a longer period of time, I'm doing one movie now and another two years later, god willing."

Director David Carson, who worked closely with Berman on the DEEP SPACE NINE pilot, "Emissary," said of the executive producer, "Rick has always encouraged very individualistic approaches from the directors. That's why you don't constantly see the bridge looking the same and you try to find different ways of doing it. Rick's idea is to have different directors with different viewpoints creating different looks and different styles, which gives the director far more freedom than you normally find in episodic television. You're allowed the freedom to create and, quite frankly, such directing is not encouraged on other shows."

With one year under his belt of launching a new STAR TREK television show, Berman says it's difficult to compare producing the two series. "It's like the difference between asking me how I felt about my first kid compared to my second kid," said Berman. "THE NEXT GENERATION was my first year with STAR TREK. It was a learning experience, it was a mess. It was chaotic, there were a lot of conflicts on the writing staff and no one knew what was going to happen. DEEP SPACE NINE's first season, on the other hand, has run like a fourth season show — it has been smooth and it has been peaceful and I'm much more comfortable.

"Creativity on NEXT GENERATION grew greatly from 'Encounter At Farpoint' to the end of the season," continued Berman. "I think DEEP SPACE has perhaps grown more. When you're living in a world of chaos — as we were in the first season of the NEXT GENERATION — it's hard to be reflective, it's hard for everybody to work smoothly. Everybody was new to it. Here we managed to have such a smooth running machine both in terms of the production and experienced directors and writers. I think it gave us all more of an opportunity to sit back and fine-tune and try and make DEEP SPACE NINE better. First season of NEXT GENERATION was more like treading water and getting through it, but they both have evolved in their own ways and, ironically, now in its sixth season going into its seventh, the NEXT GENERATION is as smooth running a machine as anybody would ever want to have."

Despite criticism of NEXT GENERATION's idea of alien cultures being people with funny foreheads and crinkly noses, Rick Berman is adamant about preserving the integrity of his perception of what Roddenberry's 24th century should be. While it occasionally upsets members of his staff who want to experiment with bolder ideas, they respect his vision. "STAR TREK, by definition, is hokey," said Berman. "We have costumes which are obviously science-fiction costumes and make-up, but it's very important to me that make-up and prosthetics don't look like masks from a really classy Halloween store. I don't want creatures to look like monsters. I don't want people dressed like 1950's sci-fi spacemen. People flying around in space suits and in starships going at speeds faster than light and speaking perfect English and nicely breathing the same air and walking around with the same gravity is preposterous, but it's a world we've all come to accept and use for a variety of metaphorical and entertaining reasons.

Because the premise is somewhat outlandish, it is essential that the specific elements within it have to be grounded in very believable reality. Our characters have to deal with each other in a very believable and realistic way. The hokiness elements for me are almost moreso in story and script than anywhere else. The one major input I put into the scripts tend to be after they have been beat out and written and have to deal with dialogue and plot points. They have to deal with keeping the dialogue believable and logical and not melodramatic and not contrived and keeping the stories clear and keeping it from being swords-and-sorcery, which is a word Gene loved to use, and stay away from hokey and corny melodrama."

THE OFFICIAL STAR TREK

FAN CLUB OF CANADA ™

Volume 1 Number 1 / Winter 1993 – $5.95

TREKKING WITH STAR TREK: DEEP SPACE NINE

On the set with Canadian director Paul Lynch

A checkup with DS9 doctor, Siddig El Fadil

Behind the scenes with makeup master Michael Westmore

Plus much more

CHAPTER THREE

MICHAEL PILLER: THE MAN WITH THE GOLDEN PEN

DEEP SPACE NINE was spared the early staff rivalries that typified THE NEXT GENERATION's early season, which included former TREK writers like David Gerrold and D.C. Fontana and television veterans like Robert Lewin and Herb Wright all railing against Gene Roddenberry's extensive rewriting of their episodes. DEEP SPACE NINE began the season with a small staff that had already been advised by Executive Producer Michael Piller that he was looking to imprint his vision on the scripts and would be involved in extensive rewriting of the teleplays.

When Michael Piller assumed the reigns of leadership over THE NEXT GENERATION's writing staff third season, he eschewed the emphasis on action/adventure storylines and focused instead on character-driven drama. It's a philosophy he carried over to DEEP SPACE NINE as well.

"There isn't a show that goes by that doesn't have something to do with one of our characters," said Piller. "My first thought was I've got to define these characters. I want the writers to know who they are and I want the audience to know who they are. If I can define them, then step one has been accomplished. People keep telling me that writers find me intimidating, and it might be because I'm just a bastard, I doubt it. My instinct is that it is because I set

extraordinarily high standards for myself and for the staff to do the best possible work they can. Rick Berman said in the middle of the season, 'It must be very miserable being you and waking up each morning and being as negative about your work as you are.' I have a very high standard and I feel we've succeeded in meeting it on DEEP SPACE NINE."

Another daunting challenge for Piller was living up to the expectations of the audience after the airing of "Emissary," the well-received pilot which appeared to redefine the nature of televised science-fiction by presenting feature quality effects and production values coupled with challenging philosophical underpinnings. "It wasn't until I saw the first two episodes on film that I began to worry there might be a letdown and that might be the challenge," said the writer. "Looking at the first two episodes, I said they're television shows. The pilot was not a television show, I don't know what it was, it wasn't exactly a movie, so I was a little worried there was going to be a letdown and I think there has been. But I think once people accept it's a television show — and a really good one — that those feelings will be overcome."

Piller acknowledged the high expectations for the series by viewers were aspirations for the show shared by himself and the writing staff. "My job, as I defined it to myself, was I had to do 18 hours of quality television. I have to launch this series creatively from a writing standpoint the best I possibly can week after week.

I don't have to get it wrong and then get it right. I've got to get it right, that's my challenge. That meant I was going to do a lot of writing this year on the show. I had the very able assistance of Ira Behr, who saved my bacon more than once, and some lovely work by Peter Fields and two very good story people, Robert Wolfe and Evan Somers. But I told Ira when he came, 'You have to know I'm going to be doing a lot of the writing this year because I want it to be right and that's just the way the first season was going to be.' That was the challenge: to make the quality of the show up to THE NEXT GENERATION quality."

Piller's continuing association with STAR TREK has resulted in a multitude of new opportunities, including convention appearances, honors at humanitarian dinners, interviews for both broadcast and cable television, and perhaps strangest of all, the chance to host a segment of QVC's TREK home shopping hour. "I think everyone should be on the home shopping network once," Piller smiled. "I was proud to be a member of the STAR TREK HOME CLUB. It was great, I would be sitting there saying how DEEP SPACE NINE was committed to protecting the vision of Gene Roddenberry and that he sits on our shoulders everyday and that we believe that the optimism and the vision of Roddenberry was the most important thing that we could preserve on the new show — and then the guy would come on and say 'And that vision is on the back of this sweatshirt here, ladies and gentlemen...'"

The new generation of STAR TREK heroes **VOLUME 2**

STAR TREK

DEEP SPACE NINE

THE OFFICIAL MAGAZINE

Published by **STARLOG**
K49127

EXCLUSIVE INTERVIEW

AVERY BROOKS

COMMANDING THE SPACE STATION

DEEP SPACE THOUGHTS FROM CO-CREATOR RICK BERMAN & THE CAST

DISPLAY UNTIL MAY 11, 1993

$4.95 US $5.95 CANADA

BONUS POSTERS: The Aliens of DEEP SPACE NINE!

CHAPTER FOUR

WELCOME TO BAJOR

Working for Berman and Piller was a small staff of veteran professionals and two writing newcomers. Leading the staff were Peter Allan Fields, who had most recently been an Executive Script Consultant on THE NEXT GENERATION, and Ira Steven Behr, a former NEXT GENERATION writer/producer, who had spent the last several years working on feature screenplays. Said Behr, "I started work on June 8th and on June 12th there was a memo that Peter and I gave to Michael that had the premises for 'Dax,' 'Captive Pursuit,' 'Babel,' and one other. We had the core right off the bat. That wasn't the problem, the problem was that we didn't know enough about the show to do it because we had so little to go on. We had a rough spot somewhere within the season and no stories came in for two months, which was a little tough but we started off okay."

The close-knit staff which worked in concert with Michael Piller found themselves getting along extremely well, although without a completed pilot script and a set cast, the work proved extremely difficult at first. Fields, the television veteran, regaled the two younger writers with stories from his career during which he crossed paths with virtually every major talent in Tinsletown. "I'm so old by now that my contemporaries and friends are historical legends to half of these guys," laughed Fields.

"We started the first season with me and Peter alone in a room together having to meet each other, not knowing each other," said Ira Behr. "Our only link was he wrote for the MAN FROM U.N.C.L.E. and I watched THE MAN FROM U.N.C.L.E."

Said Fields, "When I came aboard, the writing wasn't finished and I was all alone here except for Michael and Rick, so I didn't get that much done."

Even in its earliest stages, both Berman and Piller believed that DEEP SPACE NINE's advantage over NEXT GENERATION was its ability to allow for interpersonal conflict by putting Federation personnel in an alien environment with feuding non-Federation species. It's a feeling that is echoed by first year staff writer and former NEXT GENERATION intern, Evan Somers. "In order to develop that kind of conflict over time and for it to end up not seeming contrived, they had to come up with high concept material to create conflict between characters and guest stars on THE NEXT GENERATION. It's very high concept, science-fiction oriented and very clever. We didn't need to try that hard on DEEP SPACE NINE because we have conflict built in. We have a station that, if not monitored carefully, can shake apart at the seams and we've got controlled conflict even among our senior officers. It's more a matter of controlling potential conflict rather than seeking it out."

Added Somers, "I think the diplomatic/military chain of command aboard the Enterprise is more formalized. We've got Quark who is a merchant with questionable morals. We've got Odo who adheres to no man's laws, just the purity in truth of seeking justice in the face of others trying to buy him out and compromise his values. He doesn't represent Bajor or the Federation but a higher set of values. We've also got Sisko who seems rather isolated there on the station, which is different from NEXT GENERATION — which is the Federation on wheels. There's no one on the Enterprise that isn't a Starfleet officer, so they all have the same goals and are willing to cooperate to the same ends."

Not everyone agrees that the NEXT GENERATION formula was any more constricting. Said Peter Allan Fields, "I know that's the popular belief. I don't feel that way at all. I felt it was as easy or as difficult to write a dramatic scene on the Enterprise as it is on Deep Space Nine. If you get two guys in a compartment of a vessel, whether it's Ten Forward or on the Promenade, you have two people facing each other with a dilemma, a problem. It doesn't matter whether you're in space or in Disneyland or your mother's kitchen, it's either good or it's not."

By combining character development with action / adventure, DEEP SPACE NINE quickly latched onto a formula that helped distinguish its first season, making it one of personal satisfaction for those who worked on it. "It was a better ride for me than I had any right or reason to expect it would be," said Peter Fields. "You get into a formula sometimes, the obligatory scenes. We haven't found that on this show. Every script is not fun, because some of them are too hard to be fun, but looking back at them is fun. There's been great diversity and we've had a chance to explore the characters as much as I thought we could and find facets of them that I really think portend great interest for the future. We will slowly flesh out our characters both for the audience and for ourselves. That is much more interesting than writing the same cops and robbers show every week. I'm very happy here. You're not supposed to be and I am. Cynicism decrees that I am supposed to say something acerbic but I must tell you its a joy. It's a hard job, but its a joy."

In assessing the season, Michael Piller believes that the 18 episodes can be divided into three distinct groups of shows, initially driven by their desire to define the characters. "The first eight to ten shows were specifically designed to elaborate and expose the audience to each one of the characters," said Piller. "If you went through them show by show, you could see one was an Odo show, another

a Dax show, an O'Brien show, etcetera. We wanted to really define those characters in a way the NEXT GENERATION never did the first two seasons. We wanted those characters known to the audience right off the bat. We couldn't do it all in the pilot. We did Sisko in the pilot, we did some Kira in the pilot and then each one after that exposed more of the characters."

Continued Piller, "The next group of shows are trying to show two things; how the ensemble will work together and how far the series can stretch its wings. Then you have a third part of the season which is paying the cost for the first two thirds. The shows at the end of the season were not bad shows by any means, but were designed specifically to pay back some of the bills that we owed."

"The character things are always the best to write," said Ira Behr. "The character stories to me are always intriguing. It's tough to find

character stuff in 'If Wishes Were Horses' or 'Move Along Home,' it doesn't mean they're not good shows, but in terms of the writing that's probably why I don't like 'The Passenger', it's not really that character-oriented. I don't have that visceral hold on it."

"Zooming through the starscape is fine, but it doesn't mean anything," agreed Fields. "I've been lucky in that I'm not very good at the technical stuff and the shows that I've been able to do this year have been basically either one on one shows or internal. A lot of STAR TREK fans don't like that kind of thing and it's their prerogative, but I do that better than I would do a technical story."

The Making of the
Four Star Trek Pilots

Steven Spielberg's
seaQuest DSV

An Exclusive Interview with
Clive Barker

Demolition Man
Sylvester Stallone

The Behind-The-Scenes Story of
Batman: The Animated Series

A Farewell to
Quantum Leap

ROBOCOP
The TV Series

Lois & Clark:
A Superman Preview

Cadillacs and Dinosaurs
Preview the New Animated Series............

CHAPTER FIVE

SINGING THE SOUNDSTAGE BLUES

In the same way that the writers embraced the dramatic character differences that distinguished DEEP SPACE NINE from THE NEXT GENERATION, the series directors were thrilled to find themselves at work in a new venue as well. Said NEXT GENERATION and DS9 helmer Winrich Kolbe, "It's more intriguing, at least right now, because it's new. Since the sets are different, I am finally getting to have colors, textures, depth and foreground pieces in ops. You've got a lot more angles to work with."

Kolbe, better known as "the Barron," is equally enthused about the new ensemble that has been assembled. "The cast is terrific. I've worked with Avery Brooks before, and when I heard that Avery was doing the show, I said good. It's not going to be easy. Avery is not an easy person, but he's a damn good actor and a top notch professional. We worked together quite well on SPENCER: FOR HIRE and on HAWK, and I think he's going to bring this show to about the same heights as THE NEXT GENERATION. And then Nana Visitor plays an obviously marvelously quirky, antagonistic character. She is a lot of fun to work with. The characters are more interesting than in STAR TREK. They are so far out. You really can push them."

For Rick Berman, Herman Zimmerman was a natural choice for designing the new show's alien look and his close collaboration with the production designer and Piller has helped firmly entrench DEEP SPACE NINE as the cutting edge of televised science-fiction, simultaneously allowing Zimmerman creative freedom. "Herman and I have been close for many years,, even after he left the show [NEXT GENERATION]," said Berman. "I knew I wanted to bring Herman into this from the start and the exterior of the station was something that we spent a lot of time on. There were dozens of designs, most of which I didn't like. Some of which Michael liked and I didn't, others I liked and Michael did. Finally, we came up with an idea that worked very nicely and constantly changed that. As far as the interior designs, we knew we wanted the Promenade and a big area that had all the shops and stores and had a bar. We let Herman go about his magical way."

Like THE NEXT GENERATION, DEEP SPACE NINE shoots on three soundstages on the Paramount lot, occasionally venturing off the studio grounds for location shooting. The station's operations center, which boasts a science station, the Cardassian equivalent of the captain's ready room, a replicator, transporter pad and environmental controls, is located on Stage 4 along with crew quarters, station corridors and the stations docking bay and launch pads. Adjacent to Stage 4 is the home of the station's Promenade housing the sexual holosuites and Quark's bar.

"It's a space station that's in a way smaller than the Enterprise," said Zimmerman. "It occupies a larger volume of space but the actual structure is mostly space and not interior volume. It has the sense of being more enclosed except for the Promenade which is a larger stage. It's more like the interior of a submarine, a nice atomic submarine mind you, but a submarine nonetheless."

On Stage 17, in addition to Quark's three-story bar and the Promenade are the sexual holosuites, where inhabitants of the station can go to satiate their erotic desires. "They are like the holodeck of NEXT GENERATION and we can program pretty much any kind of experience for any kind of location we want to but what we are doing on DEEP SPACE NINE series that we weren't able to do on NEXT GENERATION is we see the inside of the holodeck and see the machinery that runs it," said Zimmerman. "When we did NEXT GENERATION we were in a budget constraint that made us do a set that is a wireframe look, it's a grid of squares when the holodeck is not activated and they just see a black void with yellow grids. In the Cardassian holodeck when the lights go off, so to speak, you see the machinery that creates the imagery. It's a step forward for us and it's something we've always wanted to do on NEXT GENERATION and we were never able to achieve."

However, you don't need a holodeck to convince you that the illusions being created on Stage 17 are very convincing.

"You can very much lose yourself into it," admitted actress Nana Visitor who plays second-in-command Kira Nerys. "There's that slight edge of insanity which I don't know if all actors have, where you cross over into the fantasy and you're there and this is really happening and it's very easy to do on DEEP SPACE NINE on these sets."

The ship's interior design is based on the station's exterior aesthetics established by Zimmerman, which exist as four enormous miniatures, the largest of which is 6' x 6' and used by Visual Effects Supervisor Rob Legato [Legato has subsequently left DS9 and joined James Cameron's Digital Domain. TNG veteran Dan Curry will take over as FX Supervisor on DS9's second season] and his team in creating the optical effects.

"The exterior of the miniature of Deep Space Nine is composed of three concentric horizontal rings," said Zimmerman. "The outer ring is a docking ring, the middle ring is an environment and cargo ring and the center ring is the Promenade and the power core of the station. The operations center is on a pedestal that's attached to the center of the power core. The Cardassians like things in three, according to our philosophy, so there are three concentric rings and on the outside ring there are three vertical pylons that are docking pylons. The vertical pylons are also docking positions and at the very end of each of the pylons are weapon banks, phaser and photon torpedo locations, which are arranged

mathematically in such a way they make a very pleasing exterior shape seen from a distance. Any fan should be able to recognize the shape of Deep Space Nine the way they recognize the exterior shape of the Enterprise."

It is the job of the production team of the show, along with the series directors and actors, to capture that reality week after week so that viewers at home can find themselves as immersed in the STAR TREK universe as those who work everyday on its many sets. However, compared to THE NEXT GENERATION, DEEP SPACE NINE presents its own unique brand of challenges and complications.

"It can be frustrating for a director because there is more prosthesis makeup, for instance," said Supervising Producer and part-time director David Livingston. "If one person isn't ready one time you just wait, and that's the director's time. The sets are more difficult to shoot than THE NEXT GENERATION and they take longer to shoot because some of them are multi-level, the lighting is darker and moodier and they are just more difficult and time consuming to shoot."

Another complication is the fact that the crew is not as familiar with the DEEP SPACE sets as the NEXT GENERATION production team after six years. "That adds a 'burden' to the director because it takes away their time," said Livingston. "The first season everyone is still getting to know these sets. Walls that should be wild aren't wild yet. Some of the design elements

that Herman built, as you know, are unbelievable sets. They are smaller, in general, than THE NEXT GENERATION, which gives them a better look because you see more detail, people are forced together and there are weirder angles. But it more challenging to shoot them."

The differences from NEXT GENERATION however are what make DEEP SPACE NINE's sets unique. Even those viewers who may not be taken with the show's storylines, would find it difficult not to be awed by its production design. Said Director of Photography Marvin Rush, who joined the DEEP SPACE crew after having worked on NEXT GENERATION since third season, "I think the most significant thing is that the requirement was to make it look different. It was a conscious choice. Obviously, the fact that it's a meaner spirited place is reflected in the architecture — it's got a lot of hard, angular edges. If you think of the Federation of being normal looking, Deep Space Nine has got a very different geometry to it and the color scheme of the walls are much darker. The feeling of the set is more foreboding, which plays into the lighting style for me. One of the techniques I've used was to make sure the show had more contrast. If you compare them, the bridge of the Enterprise has a big soft white dome over it and it creates an office building kind of feel to it, like any conventional interior today. When you see that you pretty much have to light it that way because it drives the choices."

Nana Visitor (Major Kira Nerys) at a recent "Star Trek" convention (photo copyright © 1994 Karen Witkowski)

Rush's lighting scheme reflects the differences between the darkness of DEEP SPACE and the brighter, more pristine look of Starfleet in THE NEXT GENERATION. "In this set, we use much darker and more sinister lighting," he said. "We use more harder, less diffused light. There are more areas where light is lower and people coming in and out of light. Overall, it's more contrasty. All these things create an additional sense of contrast and more tension. As we've gone along, the station has become more familiar to our audience, and also to our cast, so ops has become a little less contrasty. In the pilot it was broken down and wasn't working. Now ops is a little bit more elevated [in terms of lighting] and that gives me somewhere to go when the station becomes in jeopardy. When there's jeopardy you want more contrast to give a sense of danger."

Another aspect of the production design that distinguishes DEEP SPACE NINE from its sister series is the fact that most of its sets are smaller than those on NEXT GENERATION. While ops and the Promenade are vast, the corridors, quarters and ancillary sets, including the swing sets used for planetscapes,, are more compact which have resulted in the directors using longer lenses to compensate to give the illusion of depth. "Some of those directors use long lenses," said David Livingston. "David Carson is famous for his use of long lenses. Other directors like Corey Allen use wide angle lenses. It just depends on their particular

bent. But the sets are smaller stylistically and that's the way we're approaching the show."

Added Livingston, "The fun part is to try and do something new. Cliff Bole came up to me after doing a NEXT GENERATION telling me he was frustrated about what to do on the bridge, that there's nothing new. At some point, you just have to let that go and say, 'Okay, we're just going to go in and shoot the bridge.' But on DEEP SPACE NINE the sets offer all kinds of opportunities for a director to come in and apply their own style to shooting the sets. It does offer more opportunities although on THE NEXT GENERATION the swing sets offer that opportunity as well."

For NEXT GENERATION, Marvin Rush had devised plans for lighting the bridge. The ability to pre-light a scene resulted in a speedier shooting schedule. "On the bridge, we had Plan A and Plan B which were routine lighting set-ups based on certain given situations: where the cast was going to be and where the camera was going to be placed," said Rush. "We have an open architecture on the Enterprise where the furniture is essentially fixed. The floor level is very large and very open and unobstructed. Ops on DEEP SPACE NINE is anything but that. The potential for laying dolly track and placing the camera is much more constrained. A lot of the furniture pieces don't strike and you can't move them, they're built in. We also have multiple levels and whenever you have multi-levels the dolly track becomes a real problem. You

either spend a lot of time building platforms or you simply use where you can put camera and you don't try and do things that can't be easily done. For all those reasons, it's hard to have a 'Plan A/Plan B.'"

Another consideration in shooting the operations center on Deep Space, or ops as it is commonly referred to, is the fact that it serves the function of a variety of sets aboard the Enterprise. "This set functions as four sets; it functions as the bridge, as engineering, the transporter room and the fourth set is observation. On the Enterprise, it forms the area where they have meetings and since it has open architecture into Sisko's office, it's also like the commander's ready room. All those sets are tied into one set. It's a very busy set with lots of things visually going on."

In lighting ops, Rush has been very conscious of creating a distinct look for the command center. Due to the fact that the room also functions as engineering with large pulsating lighting pylons representing the station's power source, the look of the lighting reflects that. "One of the things we decided to do was push highlights on the show," said Rush. "There's a lot of blown out practicals. In fact, the display system, what we call the engine which are the lighted panel columns, are running right on the clip of overexposure, riding very, very hot. All those things tend to give a sense of greater contrast and greater energy to the set."

One problem many directors have encountered in shooting ops is the restricted camera movement created by the multi-leveled set, which makes it difficult to dolly within the confined area. "We're developing strategies for camera placement," said Rush. "We're beginning to learn what we did last time and have begun to do scenes similar ways. It's not as fully organized in terms of the speed as THE NEXT GENERATION was. I'm working on it. Obviously, the less time it takes me to light and shoot on our standing sets, the more time I have for the swing sets. Scenes that can be done in a quick and economical way buys me time for the scenes where the most important things are happening."

"It was always a push because given the scope of the production that they do for any one episode, there was never really enough money and you're always battling that," pointed out director Paul Lynch who directed many of the season's early episodes, including "A Man Alone," "Babel," and "Q-Less." "Strangely enough, even with the budgets they've got, they're so interested in perfection that it is very difficult to make the money stretch. It's a difficult show in those circumstances and the sets are much larger and more difficult to shoot than the sets on THE NEXT GENERATION, which are much more simple."

It had originally been intended that DEEP SPACE NINE, which has several complicated and intricately designed multi-level sets, would make greater use out of camera cranes to give the show a more fluid and expansive look, but budget realities have precluded the

opportunity to use crane shots too frequently.

"On the pilot we were using a Enlouva with a hot-head which is essentially very similar to the python and to the Lauma," said Rush of the crane first popularized by Stanley Kubrick in THE SHINING. "It's a different system but its the same concept. The problem with it is it takes time to set and make shots you can't do any other way. We're not being able to use it on the series most of the time because we just can't afford the time."

Even without a crane, most of the show's larger sets offer a variety of different options for a director. "The Promenade is a big set and it has a lot of room for staging and visual interest, so it's a pretty straight forward set lighting-wise," said Rush. "I don't have a great deal of trouble with it. It depends what part of the set we're using. We've got bridges and walkways up above and if they're not in the shot, they become my lighting tech."

What makes several of the sets unique is the fact that they are fully enclosed which means the soundstage walls are not visible and the set is constructed to completely encircle the stage. "The main challenge of sets that are 360-degree sets is that everywhere you look, the director can point the camera. Most typical TV show sets, even a lot of feature sets, end at the top of the walls. This is not a typical TV set. It has to be lit in such a way that when the director says I want to look here, here and here, you have a way of doing it."

One way that Rick

Berman and Michael Piller avoided costly delays in shooting was to only hire directors who had worked on the NEXT GENERATION. David Carson, who had helmed some of STAR TREK's most visually interesting shows, including "Yesterday's Enterprise," "The Next Phase," and "The Enemy," was picked to direct the pilot.

"The whole idea of DEEP SPACE NINE is different from the NEXT GENERATION," said Carson. "It's broken and alien and weird and peculiar and TNG is none of those things. But the sets were a little way along when I joined the project because they were so enormously complicated and cost so much money. I found I was able to make suggestions — particularly with a view of the ease of shooting the sets — which Rick and Herman liked. When you're in ops and the Promenade, they are quite difficult multi-level sets to shoot and get the most out of. Fortunately, the production was set up in such a way that for those sorts of things we could use special equipment. They were much more complicated and much more challenging than sets normally are. You can get much more atmosphere and pictorial images out of them than you can in most TV shows. Also, it has a multiplicity of images and feelings in a way that the NEXT GENERATION doesn't."

"I like that depth," said director Winrich Kolbe of Quark's three-level bar. "That set is one set I could shoot with a 20mm lens or a 17mm lens and really get something big, and I think it needs to be shot that way. It is designed in such a way that there is not a blind spot in there unless you move all the way to the end and shoot the other way. But, generally speaking, it's a set that I think should be used, and I'm trying to use it. I'm not trying to restrict myself to just the lower echelon. If there's a scene that I can shoot with a long lens from below and shooting up — having people do their dialogue, or walk and talk, or whatever, upstairs — I would do so. The depth that you have on that set, you don't have to that degree on THE NEXT GENERATION."

While Quark's bar is a brilliantly designed three level set which stretches upwards to the roof of the soundstage, the extra time it takes to move equipment and light the upper levels of the set sometimes precludes utilizing its more unique features. Said Kolbe, "What happens in episodic television, the director comes on the set and you begin to immediately zero in, if you know what you're doing, as to where can I put my camera? Where do I get maximum production value for minimum amount of production time? That usually dictates where you want to go. There are certain areas that you might love to put the camera, like in the bar for instance. I would love to always put the camera up topside and shoot down, but that will take a lot of time. We did that in one shot and we actually made it on that particular day. We were lucky, I guess. Normally it's where can I get the camera in there. There are certain areas where

you can't put the camera in. Sometimes you say, 'God, it would be nice to have the camera in here, and if I get a Python or a Lauma crane I could put the camera in there,' but that's usually the first thing that goes out of the budget. You either have a choice of that actor and that Lauma crane or that set and that Lauma crane, and usually you know pretty quickly as to what will stay and what will go."

Despite the opportunities David Carson has been denied on the one-hour episodics that he was able to avail himself to on the two-hour premiere, directing DEEP SPACE NINE has proven a continual challenge. "It's not a letdown," Carson explained. "It's just a different approach. When you do the episodic hours you are joining a team that's already up and running. As a director, you're very much a guest of the producers and the cast who are firmly in place. It's their show and you come and hopefully contribute something to that. However, when you do a pilot and are in on the ground floor of a two-hour movie, it's very different because you're helping to create the whole thing; the visual premise and concept and everything to do with it for its whole life. Coming back to do a one-hour after you've done a two-hour pilot that seems to have been relatively successful is rather like visiting old friends. Although you use a different technique for it, you're coming back to an environment you've helped to create. It's very different from being an episodic director and doing an episode of something

you haven't helped create."

Carson, who has helmed a number of pilots, was particularly enthralled with directing DEEP SPACE NINE's two hour premiere. "It was an extremely enjoyable experience," he said. "We all had a great time doing it. I always thought that the film was rare, even in STAR TREK terms, because of its philosophical content and the way it went about solving the emotional problems that it had in it. The show was very unique and very intelligent. To actually try to find a mass audience for such a complicated and complex piece of work that was challenging on so many levels made for an extremely complex pattern for the audience to follow. You would think from time to time that it was like something out of European television in its content. Is America ready for this? And is often the case, television underestimates its audience — particularly the networks. I think the success of DS9 goes another step to prove the audience is challenged and titillated by exciting and interesting and penetrating work."

Unlike in features, however, the television director's wishes are subordinate to that of the producers. "You are given your cut and you hand it over to the producers and they do what they feel they want to do with it because after all in episodic television, you're a guest and you're not the prime mover of the project as you are, often, in a feature film," said Carson. "You come in and fulfill what needs to be done and return the product to the producers and the writers who then shape it as they want to. Part of the job is not to be pig-headed about the way you see it. It's all a matter of taste and there's no real way of saying whose taste is right and whose taste is wrong, except that one believes that one's own taste always is right."

Carson's career began in England where he started sweeping theater stages, ultimately becoming artistic director of the Leeds Playhouse and Marlowe Theater in Canterbury. Eventually, he began writing musicals and plays in London and "putting them on and winning prizes in various places." Carson soon found himself working in British television where he did rock videos and daytime soaps before he began doing films, which included the critically acclaimed Jeremy Brecht Sherlock Holmes series that aired on PBS in America.

One of the rare delights on the series during the pilot was Carson's opportunity to shoot on location. "We did three days on location on the pilot," said Marvin Rush. "We shot on the beach at Leo Carillo, which has been used by thousands of productions. We did a nice job with it, it was a beautiful beach on a beautiful day with two very attractive people."

Laughed David Carson, "We had to do a tremendous amount of looping in the pilot. Even the scenes we did on the beach. I wanted a high sea in the background, but the pounding waves drowned out the dialogue, so you get all these conflicts between sound and picture which on normal

television cannot exist. On these things you make sure that the picture has all the qualities in it that you need, even though those qualities — like fire and water — make a lot of noise which interferes with the dialogue."

Additional location shooting took place at Disney Ranch for the teaser's holodeck sequence and a picnic between Sisko and his wife recreated by the wormhole aliens. "Disney Ranch had a covered bridge that's very beautiful and we shot the picnic sequence where Sisko and all the aliens are talking to him there. We also went to a baseball field right below the Jet Propulsion Laboratory in La Crescenta. It was a fairly secluded private place where we could make a late '30s baseball training facility for the pilot."

Carson was pleased to have the opportunity to take the show off the lot for the pilot. "I think it's great to be able to do that on any show," he said. "It gives it great width and breadth. If the show calls for it, and this show did, and it was very cleverly woven into the strangeness of the story. It was good that they were earth locations and as down to earth as baseball games and stuff like that. I also enjoy working on stages — if one is able to use them imaginatively where they don't look like stages. I think a stage can be as effective as a location even though sometimes people who work on stages all the time yearn to do location work."

It's an opinion echoed by TREK helmer Cliff Bole. "If I have to work on the streets of

LA again, I'm going to quit," he laughed. "I love this controlled environment. The last four years I've been doing westerns at Disney Ranch and doing STAR TREK and it's been a great environment. I love the controlled environment of the two shows."

On "Battle Lines," in which a Runabout strands Sisko, Bashir, Kira and Kai Opaka on a planet, Paul Lynch utilized Stage 18 for the planetary exteriors and caves, often lit by flickering torches. "It was a wonderful set and a combination of standing sets and of adding pieces to the standing set. We had a wonderful spaceship that had crashed into it and the Kai is fabulous. She's a wonderful actress and like a lot of these actors like Avery and Armin and Ren, she is a theater actress too. She gives a performance where part of it is the walking dead. She was such a marvelous woman as a person and a human being that it was a joy to work with her."

"It's been one of the most stress-free job I've ever had," said Nana Visitor who portrays the Bajoran attaché. "I feel almost like I've had to become an athlete with my acting in terms of always being ready and pushing through some very long hours sometimes, but like an athlete I'm all limber and ready for anything. I can hop any which way now in my mind, which is what I love to do. The show has given me opportunities to do some very fun and exciting stories.

"On a personal level, the cast members I work with everyday are wonderful.

Avery has come to mean so much to me, he's been a real influence. If this were to be it, I'd would walk away with satisfaction with my work and the real friendship of Mr. Brooks. He's really something. We talk about everything in between set-ups and he's influenced my ideas about a lot of things. It's been fun. For me to be happy in my work and with the people I work with is pretty lucky."

Shooting exterior planetscapes on stage has proven a difficult but rewarding challenge throughout the season for both the directors and Marvin Rush and his camera team.

"There's two episodes where we went on a planet," said Rush. "I think 'Battle Lines' was good, but I have a feeling 'Progress' is better from the standpoint of a believable day exterior. My favorite episode of TNG of last season was 'Inner Light,' which was an example of day exterior done on soundstage which was pretty successful. Day exterior on soundstage is a really tough thing to do, however I like it. We did night exterior on stage for 'Darmok' on NEXT GEN fifth season. There's something really interesting when you're given the task to try and make day on stage look real. It isn't always successful, but it is a challenge and I like a challenge, so I hope they don't always take that away from me because I really get a kick out of pulling it off."

The advantage to a location are the sweeping vistas they offer, acknowledged Rush. "You can't do vista on soundstage. You can try, but you can't really do it. Outside

you can have a mile of background. On a soundstage you can have at the most 75-80 feet, it's just impossible. You can simulate it, but you can't really do it. Even using all the tools, painted backings, forcing perspective using greens, smoke and all the things you can do to make it seem more faraway, ultimately it's a soundstage and you are constrained by that limit. 'Progress' would have been a different looking show if we had gone on location. I'm not sure it would have looked better. The worst case would have been to see from stage the interiors looking out the windows to a painted backing and then to cut to a location that doesn't match. It would have been worse for suspension of disbelief because the audience is more likely to pick up on a difference than they are if it's bad. If you can make it somewhat believable on soundstage and you're consistent from cut to cut to cut, the suspension of disbelief will overcome some of that. If you have a mismatch, then your eye goes, 'That's bogus.'"

Stage 18 is DEEP SPACE NINE's equivalent of NEXT GENERATION's Stage 16, best known as "Planet Hell," where the swing sets and planet exteriors are built. "We haven't given it a nickname yet," said David Livingston, who shot a huge crowd sequence from "The Storyteller" in which a menacing overhead entity threatens a Bajoran village. "We had thirty extras, wind, lighting and it had a couple of major effects going on. They were really difficult working conditions. I had to use a bull-

horn in order to communicate since I had lost my voice. It's physically very demanding on everybody to work on Stage 18. The actors had to have big wind machines blowing in their faces and it was very debilitating, but we got through it."

Added Livingston with a laugh, "It was fun. Screaming through a bullhorn is a real power trip." Michael Piller said of Livingston, "David's a wonderful director. I don't think we have a better director than David Livingston working on the series right now because he lives in the STAR TREK universe and understands it better than anyone else. He has watched the work of directors, good and bad, as I have done as a writer reading the work of writers, good and bad, and has given himself a philosophy that has served him well. He's very talented and I'm very impressed."

A problem that some directors have encountered on the show is that the heavy use of prosthetics proves constraining. "You can't get too close," said Kolbe. "I like sometimes to go into really tight close-ups, but you have to shoot them a little bit wider. That's something that I run into on every show." As a rule, the Cardassians are also shot using long wide angle lenses to achieve a certain look, partly necessitated by their complicated make-ups. Everyone is unanimous in their praise of Michael Westmore and his group of technicians, pointing out that this is simply a fact of life in dealing with such complex prosthetics.

"We've had some problems with make-up and we've been using more diffusion than on any show I've ever done," said Marvin Rush. "We've had to back off a little bit on close-ups. You can't tell on some of the more bizarre aliens because they're so removed from what we know as human. It's very forgiving, on this show you never see pieces of rubber peeling up. The real trouble is with Rene's make-up. We've had some teething problems with that and what's been on the air has been pretty satisfactory, but it's taken a lot of time and effort and a moderate amount of grief to get there. The biggest problem is that it isn't consistent from day to day. Some days it's more on the target. It's just a daunting task. It's not an easy appliance, you're asking for a smooth face. Rene is probably the most challenging one and it has taken some extra time and care."

In shooting his first episode of DEEP SPACE NINE, "Dramatis Personae," Cliff Bole consulted with some of the show's assistant directors to bring himself up to speed on the show's production routine. "I spent more time talking to the assistant directors than I did even with the producers," said Bole. "I was fortunate to get the actors together for the first time and have a read through. It just happened that they were all available at one lunch so I was able to get them around a table and we read the script. I'd love to be able to do that every time, but you can't. It's just that time doesn't allow it. My main input for the way the show was running was Marvin Rush and the two assistant directors. I really enjoyed doing it."

Rush shares Bole's enthusiasm and enjoys the opportunity to work with different directors. "They put different demands on me," said Rush. "That's one reason I've been in this line of work. I didn't want to stamp out parts of a factory, I wanted to do something that challenged me and was different every episode. New directors come in with a new idea and show you something you've never thought of before, so it's really good to have a few new faces from time to time. Jim Conway ['Duet'] came in and did a great job. He was real professional and had a difficult episode because it didn't have a lot of action or movement. It's a small story."

"It's a lot of work," said David Livingston of directing an episode of the ambitious science-fiction series. "I always say it's a lot of work and nobody believes me. But when you have to stage a whole bunch of extras and also have big explosions and things like that, it takes a lot of time. I also tend to do stuff in oners rather than a lot of cuts, and that takes a lot time to stage and make sure the camera works right. I know my deficiencies and it's that I do a lot of takes. I do ten to twelve takes a shot."

Added Livingston, sharing a STAR TREK directing secret, "What we do on the show when you go past ten or eleven takes is you change the slate number so you don't look like an idiot."

STAR TREK

THE OFFICIAL FAN CLUB

THE OFFICIAL FAN CLUB

EXCLUSIVE INTERVIEW:

RENE AUBERJONOIS

The Shape-Shifting Odo

SPECIAL FEATURE:

BRANNON BRAGA

Writing for Star Trek!

CHAPTER SIX

AS THE
SPACE STATION TURNS

"There certainly has been harmony and all of a sudden, 18 episodes have been done," said Peter Allan Fields reflecting on the completion of the first season's worth of episodes. "Usually the people on the set are clamoring for the script and you're in there burning the midnight oil doing it. On several occasions, we've had scripts ready well before shooting time even though it takes us longer to do scripts than any show I've ever worked on. I think that if we've saved time it's because of Michael and Ira and the breaking of the stories. We talk in shorthand and understand what we mean and pity the poor writer who has to sit and listen to us talk shorthand. That aside, we seem to work on the same wavelength."

Joining the writing staff first season was Robert Hewitt Wolfe, who pitched to DEEP SPACE NINE after selling the NEXT GENERATION episode, "A Fistful of Datas" and had made a major spec script sale of a science-fiction feature screenplay. Later in the year, former TNG intern Evan Somers came aboard as a staff writer at the urging of Ira Behr after doing a rewrite of "Battle Lines."

"It was originally supposed to be just Robert in my pitch meeting," said Somers. "Ira was supposed to run off to some meeting but at the last minute, he said, 'Well, it's Evan, the trainee, we owe him this' and he had somebody

waiting. He held him in abeyance and took my pitch. I got very close and there was one dissenting voice. I understood why he didn't think it would work and I left feeling there was a chance, maybe I would come back to pitch. I asked Ira if he could steer me in a more precise direction and he loaded me down with the most recent final drafts of all the episodes he had. He said they wanted more character-driven than plot-driven material, and that I tended toward the plot-driven. The next week, he calls me up and offers me a rewrite job on 'Battle Lines.' Apparently, he had really gone out on a limb for me. They hired a writer to work on it and were disappointed with his initial drafts. It was coming up on the Christmas holiday and the staff of three was tied up with other rewrites. Ira went on a limb and told Michael I could do a good job on it. I'm sure inside he was praying I could. They told me they were extremely happy with it and I got a call a few days later from Michael and he said they were going to make me an offer to come on staff. It was a miracle and since then I've come to realize this a very hard show to write for and to pull off."

The first one-hour episode of the season to go before the cameras was "A Man Alone," a murder-mystery in which Odo is accused of killing an old enemy. Work on the episode began a week after shooting on "Emissary" was completed on September 29th, 1992. Under the directorial reigns of Paul Lynch, "Man Alone" was a completely dif-

ferent type of storytelling from the pilot. "It was a very soft episode and a soft character show with some serious conflicts in it," said Michael Piller. "I wrote to be as simple and straightforward as we could do. I was thinking we had used all the effects and gags at our command in the pilot and now let's do a very simple character show and see how it plays. I also wanted to explore the idea of looking at DEEP SPACE NINE as Bochco looked at HILL STREET BLUES and that station — although I wasn't interested in doing continuing stories. I wanted to show that within the building structure of DS9, there were lots of different things happening at once with different stories that are crossing paths. I wanted to do an A/B/C story and see if we could keep them all going at one time, interacting and intersecting. That was the goal, and from a script point of view, I thought it worked quite well. On film, it flattened out a little bit. We were just right out of the pilot and were still freshman-like people in that episode."

Ira Behr doesn't feel that the show's murder/mystery storyline fell too early in the season for the then stillborn series. "We talked about that because we *are* aware of these things," he said. "We felt that what was nice about being the third STAR TREK series is that there is no such thing as early in the season, to a certain extent. You could just as easily say that 'Move Along Home' was a third season show and that you don't make your characters seem that potentially foolish the first year, but this is STAR TREK.

A group of "Deep Space Nine" alien extras enjoy a meal between set-ups during shooting of "Emissary" (photo copyright ©1994 David Strick/Onyx)

You want to believe your audience has a certain amount of sophistication, that they'll accept what you give them. It makes sense to do a murder / mystery with a character that happens to be a figure of justice and law. You want to get him involved with a murder, and what better way to show his feelings about his job?"

Unlike THE NEXT GENERATION, where "bottle shows" set exclusively onboard the Enterprise became a synonym for "money-saver," Michael Piller realized starting with the station-bound "A Man Alone" that even episodes set entirely aboard the space station didn't necessarily translate into budget savings. "I thought 'A Man Alone,' which was the simplest bottle show I could create, would be $100,000 under pattern but it was $200,000 *over* pattern. The space station also has more aliens, more costumes, more extras than we anticipated and the weren't budgeted for and so we were going over $60,000 overbudget on every episode just right off the bat; on make-ups and costumes and hair and it was a nightmare. The pilot created costs that bleeded over because we had to rebuild the sets from the pilot that had been destroyed by the Cardassians, and those costs got accrued to 'Man Alone.'"

Said Rick Berman, "This show is harder to produce than NEXT GENERATION budgetarily. You have to fill the place up with more people, costumes and prosthetics and make-ups. They end up being very expensive. It's an expensive show to shoot. We need some more money, we didn't budget make-up properly so we're always over budget in makeup. We want to do some revamping of sets as well next year and make Deep Space Nine a little bit more like a space station at the mouth of a wormhole than an elegant mall. We need the people that we see walking through the Promenade to look more like sailors off ships and less like husbands and wives on a shopping trip. That means more extras and more costumes and more prosthetics. We need to make the place busier and more active and less sterile. There's going to be a lot of work on the Promenade."

Although the first eight episodes took place largely on Deep Space Nine, the ambitious "Move Along Home" was impacted on severely by the budget woes. "I would have thought based on my NEXT GENERATION experience that at the midway point of the season I'd be in great shape," said Michael Piller. "I knew this episode was going to be hugely expensive, but I thought that I'd have money to burn because we had done so many shows on the space station."

In "Move Along Home," an alien race that is cheated by Quark transports the senior staff into an alternative reality where they must successfully complete a game simultaneously being played out in Quark's bar as they face a number of obstacles on their quest to *move along home*. "It was a killer," said David Livingston. "It came at a point in the season where we were overbudget. We didn't know how we were going to do the show. We had to make substantial changes in it and yet it was still a huge episode. David Carson pulled it off. He is a terrific director."

The episode boasted a number of intricate alien dominions, including a conclusion in which Sisko, Kira and Dax are threatened to be swallowed by a chasm when Quark elects to have his players take the dangerous path. Said Livingston, "The cave sequence at the end with the stunts was amazing. We spent a lot of time planning it along with laying the air bags that

they fell onto. It just took a lot of time and a lot of thought. We had a lot of discussion about where the chasm would be and the logic of how one person that's injured couldn't get across and the other two could. We ended up putting on a matte shot to see the chasm and it just took a lot of careful planning to make the logic of it work and then be able to make it physically inside there."

By the end of the season after several costly episodes, including "Move Along Home," "Vortex," "Battle Lines," and "The Storyteller," the producers needed to scale back their elaborate plans to bring the episodes in line with the limitations of the year's pattern budget. "'Duet' was conceived as a direct result of that very consideration," said Peter Allan Fields of his story in which Kira confronts a Cardassian war criminal. "It costs a lot to make this show and everybody does their best, but you run over and in your first year you've already had the pilot and the studio says you've spent this wad of money on the pilot, now simmer down. Of course, we have, but when you get to show seventeen or eighteen, you want your last show of the season to have some scope and so on the next to last show of this season, they said 'Pete, can you do us a favor, can you please write a show that costs nothing?' I said, 'Of course, be glad to' and then you leave the office because you've said yes to your boss and you die a thousand deaths."

Said Nana Visitor,

"'Duet' was a wonderful episode. It was kind of harrowing to have to deal with that subject matter every day, but the harder it is, the more rewarding it is. I think artistically that's always the case. When you have limitations set on you, that's when you have to start being creative. I think everyone has done that and amped up the creativity just a little bit."

"If you came to me at the beginning of the year and said by the end of the first season, you're going to be out of money to do big, sweeping shows, I would have said, get me a gun; check please," reflected Ira Behr. "But it forces you to look at the show on a different level. I'm really pleased with the mix we achieved. I felt the shows we did should be DS9-specific. To me, the episodes, good or bad, are probably shows you wouldn't do on NEXT GENERATION. These are DS9 shows and I think those are good shows to do."

In addition to budgetary constraints, DEEP SPACE NINE wasn't spared the script-crunch that has typified the STAR TREK development process over the last six years. Midseason, after going two months without buying a pitch, Michael Piller was forced to resurrect material that he had purchased for previous seasons of NEXT GENERATION, including "The Storyteller."

"This was a script that was written for NEXT GENERATION on spec by a writer named Kurt Michael Bensmiller, who wrote 'Time Squared,'" said Piller. "I've had this script in my desk for three years and I bring it out every season and I say should we do this script this year? Everybody reads it and they say, let's not do it. They just didn't like it. I needed some shows and I needed to put some things into development.

"One of the really big problems with this script, which is why it didn't appeal to anybody, is because it was not about any of our characters," added Piller. "We were just watching the events occur by putting O'Brien in the middle, saying you have to solve it. What really appealed to me was the great theme that sometime we create our own monsters so that we can defeat them and we feel secure in our power. I was always in love with that theme and, finally, we made it work. Ira did a lot of work on that script."

"I like 'The Storyteller' a lot because it gave us a chance to do Bashir and O'Brien, and that's the core of that show," said Ira Behr. "It also gives a nice little feel for the Bajorans and shows that Bajor is indeed a very strange place. There are things happening in those little hamlets and villages that are certainly not your average Federation attitude towards life, religion and spirituality. What I wanted to do was a show that explored the fact that you have two guys working together and one, Bashir, wants to have a really close relationship and the other one, O'Brien, is saying back off. This was a chance for them to get together. Colm's quite good. It's basically THE MAN WHO WOULD BE KING and he's a wonderful person to make king."

Bashir and O'Brien are paired again in second season's THE ARMAGEDDON GAME. Said writer Morgan Gendel, "We have worked out a story where you see some different shades and genuine heroism from Bashir," he said. "It's man on the lam story and, basically, Bashir and O'Brien are on the lam together. It brings in a little element of nuclear disarmament, future-style. Originally, it was going to be Dax and Bashir and you would see a new relationship grow, but they felt they had played that beat one too many times and there were some other directions they want to go with that.

"O'Brien and Bashir turned out wonderfully together because O'Brien is so closed up emotionally. He's the Sergeant Friday of DEEP SPACE NINE and so closed up, 'just the facts, m'amm' but such a terrific actor too. If you can play a situation where he has to go against that and needs the help of somebody else, or by circumstance feels the need to talk about something emotional, that's neat. Bashir has to go the other way, he's not the one you want to get stuck alone with — he's going to talk you to death and yet he has to go the other way in this story and be the strong silent type a little bit."

The changes in the characters second season reflected the fact that in year one the producers realized they were departing dramatically from they way they initially envisioned them. "Bashir was originally going to be a much more conventional character than what he turned

out to be," said Ira Behr. "I know there's been some question about Bashir being a different type of STAR TREK character and I think it's taken the audience some time to get in synch with that. I like the character a lot. Originally, he was conceived as just this kind of cocky, good looking, somewhat arrogant young doctor. What he is now is obviously more than that, whether for good or bad depends on your tastes."

Said Science Advisor Naren Shankar, who also contributed a rewrite of "Babel," "I think he has potential and I'd like to see him do some more demanding roles. It's kind of fun to see him hitting on girls all the time, but for that to be his only note is silly. I just want him to stop looking so unsure of himself. There's a difference between being cocky and unsure. This is a guy who came out of Starfleet Academy at the top of his class and he shouldn't be stammering all the time. He shouldn't be frightened by authority all the time. This is supposed to be a very competent guy and I'd like to see him grow out of that a little bit. He's a fine actor."

"It's been great," said El Fadil. "This year has been pretty much everything it could of been and everything one could have wanted it to be. The character has taken off a bit in his own way and he's getting on. He's not quite such a jerk, which is nice."

Commented Michael Piller, "One of the things about 'Past Prologue' that bothered me was that Bashir's performance was in a very broad range — and this is newness. I believe we have strange aliens, strange make-up, spaceships, explosions and wormholes and costumes that are crazy so that the people within them have to be entirely credible. If those people get too big in their performances, then you go into opera and it becomes space opera, foolish and unbelievable. Patrick Stewart really led the way with us in NEXT GENERATION, which is to underplay. When you think you're going to go big, you come down and it has much more power and credibility. You believe there's a space station or a spaceship like Enterprise. The biggest problem with the early shows is that some of the performances were too big or too restrained. We had to find the even tone for the ensemble to work together. Our voices weren't quite right and the performances were uneven. The first episode hurt the character of Bashir because he was so broad in those scenes with Andy Robinson that he looked like the greenest recruit in the history of the Starfleet, and that hurt him for two or three episodes. Now, if we were shooting it today, his performance would be much more credible and he wouldn't have the same reaction from the audience that he has now."

Bashir wasn't the only character to vary from his initial design. "Dax has obviously changed a little bit," said Behr. "She's gone away from the Trill as Mr. Spock. In a way, Terry Farrell is enabling us to make her a more interesting Trill. She has a much more interesting sex life than she was supposedly going to have, and by building the backstory on

Cruson Dax in 'Dax' it opened up the whole issue that she is not your usual Trill. She's someone who you'd find at 2 o'clock in the morning partying with a bunch of Ferengi sitting at the bar when the bar is closed, drinking and gambling, and just having a good time."

"I remember thinking about her as sort of a placid, Spock-like character with great wisdom and insight and a broad view," said Michael Piller. "Sort of Grace Kelly on a good day, but as we did more with her we got the idea that this is basically a character in turmoil with all these experiences, entities and memories, heartbreaks, disappointments and violations of trusts, which makes her a very complex character who is really, in some ways, screwed up. What she appears to be is a very placid 28-year-old woman, but in fact she has a lot of angst that comes from six lifetimes of experience. I don't know how any of us might do with that experience. She's more and more complex as we go on."

Said Naren Shankar, "I like Dax. I think that she could be as interesting on DS9 as the Vulcans were on the original. There's a lot of complexity and places to explore with these people and it would be nice to know more about their society and I think you will."

One of the most important characters for the series was its commander ("I have to stop writing Captain," laughed Piller), Benjamin Sisko, who had to have his own strong identity while remaining true to the spirit of leadership established in the two previous incarnations of STAR TREK.

"We haven't spent a great deal of time on Sisko since the pilot," said Michael Piller. "I don't think there has ever been in the history of STAR TREK a better developed character from the starting point as Sisko was in that pilot. I don't think you have ever known as much about any of the other characters on NEXT GENERATION or the original as you do about Sisko. We said a lot about him and we have not explored him in other ways. That might have been a mistake, but I wanted to see him as an officer and as a leader of an ensemble. I wanted that ensemble to work and the other people in the show to get their hour."

Avery Brooks, who portrays Benjamin Sisko, was best known as the menacing enforcer Hawk of the SPENSER: FOR HIRE ABC series and his own short-lived show, A MAN CALLED HAWK. For Brooks, the role of Hawk, which he recently reprised in a Lifetime cable film SPENSER: CEREMONY, is one that he has very strong opinions about. "While playing Hawk, I was very conscious of playing a character that by definition was mythical in dimension," said Brooks. "If you look beyond the superficiality of wearing sunglasses at night, the gun and the big car, you have the makings of the consummate blues hero.

"To be able to come into a situation — not just in the nick of time — but to come in on time and ultimately change the course of the outcome is something that I think appeals to us all as humans. In addition, the other appealing aspect of this role is the relationship between Hawk and Spenser. Despite the fact that these two men are from different races and backgrounds, they are still able to co-exist without either one betraying himself."

Said writer Morgan Gendel, "I think Sisko is a good character. He's a real rock. To me, he's like Mary Tyler Moore who was the center of THE MARY TYLER MOORE SHOW where you had all these other characters squirreling around her — but you couldn't do the show without her. To me, Sisko is the center of the hurricane."

Peter Fields would like to see more done with the character of the Commander in the future. "I think we have to have more either for Sisko or from Sisko," he said. "He's our commander and the loneliness of command and that sort of thing is all well and good, but I'd like to see him with a little more humanity and we simply have to give him that. We have to give him stories and situations which don't divest him of his command status but that let us see a little more of the guy."

"He's a different kind of commander than Picard and a different kind of commander than Kirk," said Robert Wolfe. "He is more true to the military. I think he's a good role model and a strong guy in his own right."

Avery Brooks' casting affected the portrayal of Sisko dramatically, making him much more of an officer in the Kirk vein than that of Jean-Luc Picard. "Originally Sisko wasn't going to be quite the

commander that he became," said Ira Behr. "We thought he was going to be more easy-going. Surprisingly, some of the feedback that we've been getting from people in the military is that Sisko is the closest thing to a true military commander that has yet been on STAR TREK, more than Picard, more than Kirk. They feel his relationship with his people is much more like the way the true commander of a sub or a ship would behave, which is not so much that he's by the book, but there's a formal behavior to him and an attitude and a strength that I wasn't quite thinking of."

Sisko's strong, assertive leadership is countered by his warmth as a father. "In the scenes with Jake, which I think are very successful, you see a whole different side to him," said Behr. "You see he is very soft and gentle. I really like those scenes when they're together."

"I think the importance of the scenes between Sisko and his son cannot be underestimated," added Michael Piller. "I think it's what defines him as a different kind of Starfleet hero; it makes us see how warm a character he is and I think those moments are gold. We need to build as many of those into the episodes as we can. The two of them are very good together and it's a very important relationship."

Sisko's relationship with Kira has also grown in importance over the year. It's a dynamic that epitomizes the differences between the Federation and Bajor, which also illustrates the common

bond that exists between the two peoples. Said Behr, "We've explored the relationship between Sisko and Kira in little increments and see there is a true friendship growing there. He is aware of her as a human being and not just as a subordinate or as the Bajoran Liaison or first officer. Sisko has a lot of levels both as an actor and as a character. It makes me feel comfortable about that whole seven year cycle of shows because I think there's a lot that can be done with his character."

Nana Visitor is equally pleased with the response to her character, one of STAR TREK's first strong female roles. "It's beyond pleased," said the actress. "It's so satisfying to me when I've gone to conventions and women have told me their four year old daughter — or son — pretend that they're Major Kira, and that's very satisfying because they're identifying with her. The fact that it's a woman and she's in charge is not even an issue anymore. In this last part of this season, I feel like her being a strong female isn't the issue, it's this person who is going through growth, who's made mistakes and is living a life. I think the writers and producers are letting it go to that level and not keeping me just being an archetype — they've gone beyond that and it's wonderful."

Other characters that have changed as well include Rene Auberjonois' Odo, the shape shifting security officer, who was patterned on the traditional law-enforcement icons of pop culture. "Odo was supposed to be Clint Eastwood," said Behr. "Instead, he has turned into the angriest, most neurotic, most vulnerable man in the galaxy — which I think is wonderful. It's a great character and he's just given us a lot to write. It took at least half the season for us to stop telling freelancers when they came in to think Clint Eastwood, because it's not Clint Eastwood. It's Clint Eastwood on a *very* bad day. It's Clint Eastwood who's remembering his mother used to beat him and that he had no love and he's a man with no name who wants a goddamned name and is pissed he doesn't have a name."

"Odo doesn't want to be a human being or a humanoid," said Rene Auberjonois, the talented stage and screen actor who personifies the anthropomorphisized blob of jello. "He is forced to take the shape of a humanoid because it's the only way he can function in a society that he is almost trapped in. He would like nothing more than to find out who he really is."

"I find Odo fascinating because he is the odd man out again," said Supervising Producer David Livingston. "He is like the Data character, and yet he is unique from Data in that he has emotions, but they are emotions that he tries to hide. There have been a couple of times we have touched them. I think that makes him very compelling. His search for his roots and his people, and where he came from I think makes the character quite intriguing. Now, that's on the serious side. The way Rene plays the character with such humor and charm and stature I think makes all

that interesting. People can go on a quest and they can be boring, but the way Rene plays it I think is wonderful."

"My ego is very comfortable with the fact that I think the audience likes the character," said Auberjonois of the reception Odo has received from viewers. "They love the fact that he is a shape-shifter and I do too. I love to watch it happen. As an actor, it's not the most interesting part of the character to me because I have nothing to do with it. It's done in the computer — but I love to sit at home and watch it on television. I go, 'Whew, look at that.' I'm very glad that we don't do it every single week so it doesn't become like 'Where's Waldo' in this episode."

The same questions which plague Odo are ones that Auberjonois has to ponder as the actor that plays him. The writers haven't filled him in on the missing details either. "It is a total mystery to me," he admitted. "It's just like in the pilot where I said, 'I don't know where I came from and have no idea if there are any others like me.' That mystery of that character was the thing that really appealed to me. I'm not any closer to the answer, which is just fine and dandy with me. I think that's the key to the character and it's part of what makes him interesting to the audience. It certainly makes it interesting for me to play that."

Working as part of a large ensemble has taken some getting used to though, as Auberjonois has often found Odo uninvolved with the week's action. "There have been some shows where I've

had maybe two or three lines and I stood in the wings," said the actor. "Of course, an actor wants to be busy all the time and be the center of attention, but the truth is there have been three scripts that have centered on this character; 'A Man Alone', 'Vortex', and 'The Forsaken' and those three stories have developed the character wonderfully."

Auberjonois admitted that even when he isn't at the center of the action, he's had the opportunity to watch Odo grow. "In the pilot, he appeared as a very sort of grim, rigid, unbending character with very few real emotions," said the actor. "Now the writers have introduced aspects of his personality that I think have developed the character and evolved him and allowed him to go places emotionally each week that is a joy to play. The scripts that focused on my character the most are going to be the ones that an actor thinks are his favorite episodes, but even scripts in which I really was not at all featured, there is always something. They always manage to find a new aspect of the character that I get to investigate and I'm just tickled. I couldn't be happier."

Auberjonois also spends a fair amount of time in the make-up chair where a prosthetic is applied to give his face the quality of the formless shape-changer that can't quite become completely human, and it's a process, and anonymity, he enjoys. "I have no problem with the appliance," said Auberjonois. "I taught mask work at Juliard and I studied mask work. I have performed often in masks and what Odo wears is essentially a mask. I find masks rather liberating, rather than limiting, because you can cut through a lot of crap about what your face does. It's sort of a cosmic joke, as I say to my wife, that I spent my life making funny faces and now I'm in a situation where my face is completely covered. You can tell it's me, but none of my skin is showing."

And the make-up is the one aspect of Odo's character that continues to change the most. "To be quite candid, the makeup is in evolution," said Auberjonois. "I was cast very close to the time we started shooting. There was very little time to do the kind of extensive makeup tests that are really required for something that complicated. The thing about the makeup that makes this makeup harder than almost any makeup that they're doing or have ever done is that it is smooth. There's nowhere to hide in it. There's no wrinkles or cragginess or shadows. It's not a Klingon or Ferengi or Cardassian which has a lot of bumps and grinds in it to deal with where you can hide a lot of imperfections in makeup like that. Odo ideally should be like a sand-washed pebble that you find on the beach. Now, that's very hard to do and we hadn't succeeded until the end of the season where we came very close during the final make-up test of the season."

The bickering love/hate relationship between Security Chief Odo and Quark has already distinguished itself, proving to be one of the most enjoyable aspects of DEEP SPACE NINE. "I knew that it was going to be good because I could feel it when I was working with Rene," said Shimerman. "From all the compliments about our relationship, it seems, if I may say so, that it's one of the better things on the show and I didn't think it was going to be appreciated that much. I just thought it would be one of the qualities, but now I understand it is one of *the* qualities."

Said David Carson who first discovered the chemistry between Auberjonois and Shimerman in the pilot, "It's a little bit of give and take and they are such well drawn characters who are diametrically opposite, so it is very easy for them to interact in an interesting way. They rub each other the wrong way and knock sparks with each other when they come together and the actors enjoy it."

"It's Abbott and Costello with an edge," said Robert Wolfe. "They play wonderfully off each other."

Although many assume that the relationship had been an aspect of the show Berman and Piller had devised early on, Piller admits that it was not anticipated. "The Quark/Odo relationship was not planned for," said Piller. "I saw it coming out of the pilot scripting and then 'A Man Alone.' Until that time, until those two scripts, we figured that Odo and Quark would be going one on one with Sisko a lot and that Odo and Quark would basically be enemies and guys who didn't like each other. It wasn't until I realized in the scripting of it how much they loved their Burns and Allen routines and how they really lived for them, that the voices and exchanges and the special nature of it came through. It became for us what Bones and Spock had in the original."

Said Armin Shimerman, "Working with Rene has only gotten better. It started out good and it's only gotten better because we really do understand our relationship. I said we are all learning about our characters more. I think Rene and I learned about our relationship very quickly and I think we will continue to learn more."

One of the few characters to remain true to the template set down in the series' original bible was Quark, the mischievous Ferengi merchant, although his popularity has proven surprising as Shimerman has made the groveling barkeep the first palatable Ferengi character. "Quark has legitimized the Ferengi for the first time in the history of the series," said Ira Behr. "We're able to do things with the Ferengi now and we can look at the Ferengi just as we would look at the Klingons. The Ferengi have more to them than just the fact they are greedy little buggers in space. I think that comes from Armin's playing of the character and not making him a total buffoon."

Armin Shimerman's first appearance as a Ferengi was in THE NEXT GENERATION's first season episode, "The Last Outpost," a show which did little to endear the race to its many viewers. "Some of the people who created these guys weren't necessarily high on the Ferengis to begin with either," recalled Supervising Produc David Livingston. "I don't want to over psychoanalyze this, but the Ferengi are us. They are the side of us we don't want to see, and maybe that's painful to some people. Maybe it's painful to the fans when they see themselves in it. Initially, they weren't funny. I think by playing that sort of unpleasant side of human nature in a comic way we will engage the audience more. That's one reason why Armin is becoming popular is because he can make those human foibles humorous and palatable. We see how silly we are as people. You look at Quark and you want to take him in your arms and give him a hug. Why are you such a little shit?"

Said Shimerman, "In the middle ages, they used to have the seven deadly sins and in the theater that they had people who would impersonate each of those sins, whether it was sloth or greed or pride. I think that the Ferengi are a number of those old seven deadly sins being stuck together. What they did in the medieval times is what I'm hoping they'll do on DEEP SPACE NINE, which is that by pointing out humanity's shortcomings, its nastier sides and greedier sides, we will learn to see how ugly that is and perhaps we'll learn to eschew it in our own lives."

Offered director David Carson, "The thing about Armin's Ferengi is that he seems to have more facets than we've seen in the Ferengi. Not only is he cunning and all, but Armin has a power to him that makes him more dangerous and more threatening even

though he's still a sort of nasty little Ferengi. He has a side that's very hard and tough and would make anybody think twice about attacking this guy. Sometimes the Ferengi are played without that toughness and played as these crafty, sly we'll-do-anything-for-a-buck types and Armin is that, but he also has this tough side which means it's wrong for him to go over the top in that way — and he never has. His instincts have kept him well back from the edge."

One realization Shimerman quickly made was that when working in a large ensemble, your character won't always be in the spotlight. "As the season came to an end, I had less and less to do," he admitted. "And it was a lesson for me. I was sort of spoiled in the middle part of the season because there was so much of Quark being used. In fact, there was a period of time when I was complaining that I was being used too much, because the makeup was causing me never to get my 12-hour turnaround. I was getting no sleep whatsoever. But I sort of got used to that and spoiled by that. And towards the end of the season. when I began to work maybe one day an episode, I had some problems with that. I like work, I have a great time working. It's a lot of fun. So they were taking my play toys away from me and I was a little distraught, mixed up and unsettled at that. And as the episodes went by, I came to realize that I am part of the ensemble and I'm also not part of the Federation. STAR TREK is intrinsically stories about the

core group which on DEEP SPACE NINE is Sisko, Dax, Bashir and O'Brien. Major Kira is certainly part of that command group and Odo is needed for his qualities as well. Quark is not a part of that Federation team and so it's harder and harder. I became a writer for a moment and saw how difficult it was to include me as much as I was before and that was an education for me. I came to realize that like Worf from the other show, there will be episodes where I'm central, where I'm very important, but for the most part I should get used to the fact that I'm the second team, I'm not the first team. I'm important on the bench, but I'm not going to go in and play every game."

Said Co-Producer Peter Allan Fields, "Armin Shimerman has got Quark down and it's very difficult to make a likable character out of someone like that. This is not the dance hall girl with a heart of gold, this is a Ferengi. It's not that everything has to be for profit. He's got feelings, but they're not the same values we have, and Armin Shimerman has done a wonderful job of making a ludicrous, on the line of being cartoonish character, into a genuine vehicle for dramatic as well as fun stories."

Another character that has taken the writers by surprise was Rom, Quark's brother, played by Max Grodenechik who was the other actor being considered for the role of Quark initially. "We liked both actors who read for Quark and we felt we needed the stronger presence to deal with Sisko on a contin-

THE DEEP SPACE LOGBOOK

uing basis," said Piller. "At the same time, Max is funny and we decided when we made Nog a nephew as opposed to a son, we needed a brother to be a son to and I think it's worked out very well."

Much to Shimerman's delight, Grodenchik has become a regular staple on the show. "When Max and I were auditioning for Quark, we both thought that if we didn't get Quark, that Rom would be a good part to play, and it's worked out that way. Max is playing Rom and we're having a good time together and in 'The Nagus' episode, he had a chance to kill me and fulfill whatever fantasies he had," laughed Shimerman.

"I love the relationship between Rom and Quark," said Ira Behr. "Even though we play it for comedy, it's not easy being a brother, and brothers can be very different people and yet you're tied together in this somewhat of a love/hate relationship. We envisioned Rom as a straighter character. He was just a no-good Ferengi when he was originally conceived and now he's become a buffoon and also a figure who is a man with desires. He wants to have a piece of the pie, he would love to own Quark's and we're going to be doing stuff with him and Nog. Nog obviously has a hard time dealing with Jake's relationship with Sisko, which is so much better than what he has with *his* father. That's the other relationship that took us most by surprise. We had no idea what we were going to do with Jake, but Jake and Nog make wonderful B-stories and we'll

explore them again. It gives you a chance to do some humor and it's another level you're not used to seeing on STAR TREK. Before on STAR TREK, kids were Wesley. They were still Starfleet and these kids are anything but Starfleet, they're kids. They're trying to hangout, they've got their spot on the upper level of the Promenade. I think it's just a good color to add to the mosaic of the station."

Said Michael Piller of the two kid characters, "I always saw the Jake and Nog relationship as being an interesting and important component of this series." David Livingston first established their hangout on the Promenade based on Ira Behr's stage directions in "The Nagus," an area that has become a recurring motif in the show when the two youths sit down there in "The Storyteller" waiting for arriving women to disembark.

Behr firmly established Rom along with Jake and Nog's relationship in "The Nagus," an episode in which Quark is offered the chance to divvy up shares in the wormhole, prompting his brother to plot an assassination attempt. Some have cited "The Nagus" as STAR TREK's first attempt at comedy since the original's "A Piece of the Action."

"I think we've done a lot of comedy this year and it

does not stick out because it's part of the things we do," said Ira Behr. "It's prevalent in almost every show. Comedy to DS9 is to me what it was to HILL STREET BLUES, which always had comedy involved in it. It's just part of the scenery. I don't have a fear of doing it on that level. David originally pitched the story as a bunch of villains, thieves and scoundrels getting together to divide up the wormhole, which was an interesting story. I thought it would be too nebulous and you'd have to create too may different types of villains, so we decided to make it the Ferengi. I wasn't a big Ferengi fan, but we decided to concentrate on the Ferengi, and it just steamrolled from there. I thought the whole episode had to do with fathers and sons as much as anything else. To me, when Zek says its like talking to a Klingon, about his son, I didn't mean that as a comedy line. I wanted to define the father as having a genuine disappointment in his son who doesn't get the finesse it takes to be a Ferengi. He is as disappointed in his son as Sisko is proud of Jake by the end of the episode."

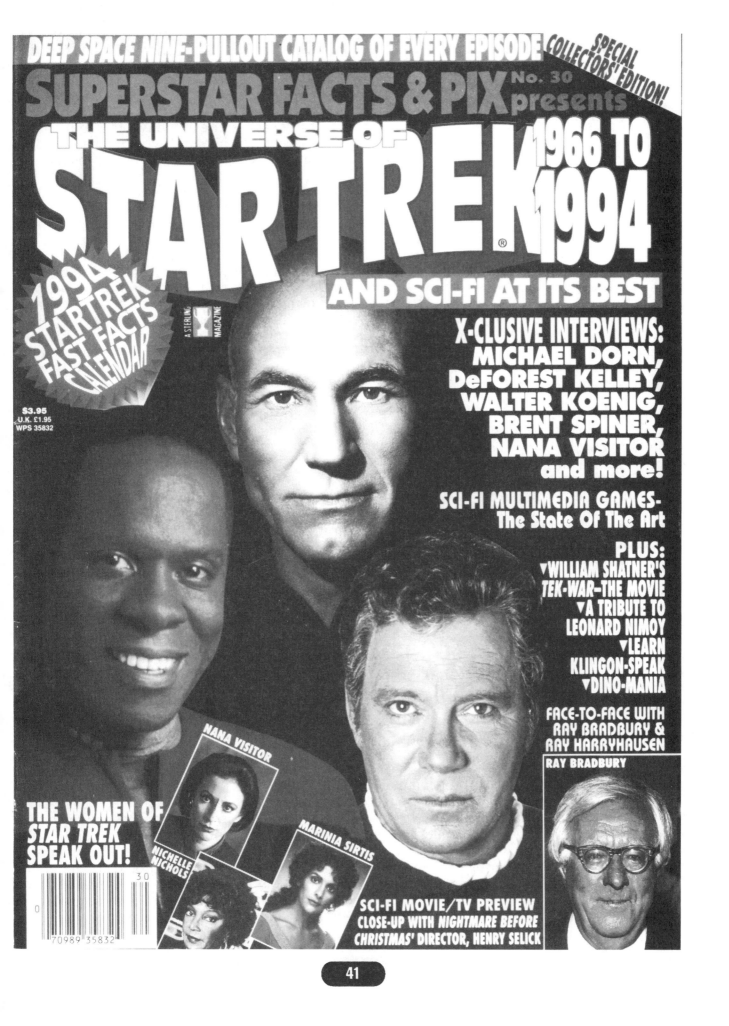

DEEP SPACE NINE-PULLOUT CATALOG OF EVERY EPISODE

SPECIAL COLLECTORS' EDITION!

SUPERSTAR FACTS & PIX
No. 30 presents

THE UNIVERSE OF
STAR TREK
1966 TO 1994
AND SCI-FI AT ITS BEST

1994 STARTREK FAST FACTS CALENDAR

A STERLING MAGAZINE

$3.95
U.K. £1.95
WPS 35832

X-CLUSIVE INTERVIEWS:
MICHAEL DORN,
DeFOREST KELLEY,
WALTER KOENIG,
BRENT SPINER,
NANA VISITOR
and more!

SCI-FI MULTIMEDIA GAMES-
The State Of The Art

PLUS:
▼WILLIAM SHATNER'S
TEK-WAR–THE MOVIE
▼A TRIBUTE TO
LEONARD NIMOY
▼LEARN
KLINGON-SPEAK
▼DINO-MANIA

FACE-TO-FACE WITH
RAY BRADBURY &
RAY HARRYHAUSEN

RAY BRADBURY

NANA VISITOR

THE WOMEN OF
STAR TREK
SPEAK OUT!

MICHELLE NICHOLS

MARINIA SIRTIS

SCI-FI MOVIE/TV PREVIEW
CLOSE-UP WITH *NIGHTMARE BEFORE
CHRISTMAS'* DIRECTOR, HENRY SELICK

CHAPTER SEVEN

GET THEE TO THE GAMMA QUADRANT

One issue that has provided a source of disagreement on staff and in viewer circles has been whether DEEP SPACE NINE's stationary venue has proven too claustrophobic, warranting further exploration of the Gamma quadrant, the unexplored territory existing on the other side of the wormhole. "By the sixth or seventh episode, I wished we had done more at the beginning of the season that took us off the station," admitted Michael Piller. "That is part of the shakedown cruise. We thought this would be a different kind of series where you'd have such an interesting setting and cross-section of personalities and aliens that you would want to be doing more shows that explored the community of the space station; that it would provide enough color to support those stories. In a sense, we were looking at that to see if it was going to work and I think it does, but we have learned that we must mix in more trips through the wormhole and more exploration of the Gamma quadrant and more trips down to the Bajoran moons."

"We've got to get out into the Gamma quadrant more and take a look around," said Peter Fields. "We've done perhaps too good a job of establishing Deep space Nine as a venue. We've got a wormhole next door and I think this next season we'll go

through it more and learn more about it. I think that's necessary to the growth of the show. We must do that or things will stagnate. It's fine to sit, but any view can get boring, or at least tedious, and we'll get on each other's nerves unless we do some real exploring."

Ira Behr disagreed vehemently, feeling that the station offers ripe opportunities for exploration within its own confines, "I hear people talk about that and I know Michael talks about that and I just don't agree. I feel the season was [set-up] to establish Deep Space Nine. In 'Progress,' 'Storyteller,' 'Battle Lines,' 'Vortex,' 'Move Along Home,' we get off the station a lot. I think that's enough for the first season of eighteen episodes. This is a whole different beginning to a STAR TREK series than what we've seen before, and I think we had to really try and hit that home as much as possible. We can only have two new sets and on NEXT GENERATION they could keep switching back to the Enterprise, which is hovering right overhead. What we're going to have to do, though we haven't done it in the first couple of shows, is keep cutting back through the wormhole to the station and do a different B-story there since you're not going to be in communication through the wormhole."

Behr attributed the criticism of the show's immobile nature to the fact that the station's diversity has failed to be exploited to its full potential. "I think people are a little bit disappointed because the station has not done everything that we wanted it to do. The

Promenade is still a problem, it doesn't have the feel that I hoped it would have. It's still too Starfleet clean for me. It needs work and hopefully more work will be done on it. I think we can continue to explore the workings of the station. We tried it a little bit at the beginning of the season which is what is day to day life on the station like — besides ships coming and going. That's something we'll continue to explore as well. There is a lot of stuff to do and as long as we go through the wormhole and have those kind of adventures, I think it's fine that we're stationary."

"I think we're leaning towards more exploration of the Gamma quadrant," said Evan Somers at the end of the first season. "It's been a proposal of Robert's that we consider acquiring a larger exploratory vessel, something with a captain's seat that Sisko can command from. I don't know where that will go. I think that could be very helpful."

Admitted Ira Behr, even when the show has gone through the wormhole, the results were often disappointing as was the case in "Vortex," where Sisko encounters an alien race over the Runabout's viewscreen that was all too human, both in appearance and in attitude. "We were not happy with that scene," he pointed out regarding that sequence in which the guest star was recast to no avail. "To me, the Gamma Quadrant should be the great unknown. If we ever get too close to any of these cultures, to me the mystery of the Gamma quadrant has been solved. We have to be very careful with what goes on with the Gamma quadrant. I like it in theory. But I'll let you know, ask me again next year."

Another hope is to delve more into the alien cultures the crew has encountered. "I think DEEP SPACE NINE will really explore the Cardassians in the future in the way the NEXT GENERATION did the Klingons," said Robert Wolfe. Added Ira Behr. "We're going to have to explore what Cardassia is. Not every Cardassian is the same. We're going to do a lot of things with the Bajorans and their spiritual and political sides. Hopefully, we can do the same thing with the Cardassians. I'd like the Cardassians to be a little more specific than the Romulans. I tend to think as the Romulans as a group, they're the Romans, the Nazis. I think the Cardassians we can show is not a planet of goosestepping males. "

Naren Shankar points out the Cardassians have evolved as a race since their introduction in NEXT GENERATION's "The Wounded." "'Chain of Command' was the beginning of our attempt to turn the Cardassians into sort of our Nazis," he said referring to TNG's take on the villains. "They're vicious and real nasty. If you take a look at 'The Wounded', they are different. They are not nearly as malevolent as they are now."

A STAR TREK tradition that DEEP SPACE NINE didn't adhere to is ending the season with a cliffhanger. One storyline originally considered was a cross-over between THE NEXT GENERATION and DEEP SPACE NINE in which they

A group of "DS9" extraterrestrial cronies pose for the camera (photo copyright © 1994 David Strick/Onyx)

faced a menacing intergalactic invasion force. Vetoed by Rick Berman, Michael Piller instead wrote a story that "bookended" the season, addressing several residual themes raised in the pilot involving the Prophets in the wormhole and Bajor. This gave the season a story arc that hadn't necessarily been planned.

"That was something Michael was insisting on and it was clever of him to want to do that," said Ira Behr. "It's a good Kira story and it's a good

Sisko story. I know people wanted to have the big cliffhanger, but I think we're going to open the season with a bang. I love cliffhangers but they do tend to be a gimmick and unless you can find a gimmick that's going to work for you, why do it? We did not have a way to do it successfully because of the budget restraints. To say you *have* to have a cliffhanger is ridiculous and I thought this was an interesting, intelligent show that does a lot for the series."

"I don't want to make cliffhangers a way of life on STAR TREK," said Michael Piller. "I didn't feel coming off the excitement of the pilot and the newness of the series that we had to do a cliffhanger. If we had a wonderful cliffhanger that we wanted to do, I would have been behind it. We came up with one that had to do with the Cardassians deciding they wanted DS9 back and we looked at it and what it would cost to do it right. It would have required a lot of money. Being a responsible producer, I didn't feel we could do a cliffhanger, which traditionally costs at least $100,000 more, and add it to the overage we already had on this season. We already had a conceptually interesting episode that could be a season-ender that gave a completeness to the season. 'In The Hands of the Prophets' is not just another episode, it's a season-ending episode that re-examines that relationship between Bajor and the Federation and that of the relationship between Sisko and Kira, and gives us some thought-provoking drama."

Said Armin Shimerman, "I am very happy. We've brought in some darker elements towards the end and we're dealing with the problems of Bajor. It's not just about adventure. It's not just about us carrying new aliens or going to a different planet to find something. We are dealing with some social issues, which I think is great. And the best part of STAR TREK is always when it deals with social issues and philosophy."

One premise resurrected second season featured a character Michael Piller and Rick Berman originally created to serve as science officer aboard Deep Space Nine. Their original concept involved a woman who came from a planet with lower gravity, which meant that in order for her to function aboard DS9 she needed to use a jet-propelled wheelchair. The character was replaced by Dax when the producers realized that another aspect of the character's make-up would prove untenable. It was their intention that the character would be given an office in a low-gravity area of the station where she could fly. Visualizing her ability to literally soar through the air on a weekly basis would have proved a costly and difficult challenge and the character was dropped. However, Evan Somers, who himself is in a wheelchair, had been approached about using the character in a script. "I think they want her as a guest star and a potential recurring character," said Somers. "There may be the potential for her to be a love interest for Doctor Bashir."

Other storylines in development include the one that had been considered as the season's cliffhanger in which the Cardassians want the station back, as well as an episode in which a machine that Quark has bought sets up an imbalance in the subspace field affecting the fabric of casuality and random luck, thus making the Ferengi the luckiest man in the universe until things begin to go wrong. Another episode, "Playing God," involves the accidental arrival of an egg-like object which ultimately turns out to be a miniature proto-universe that begins to expand aboard the station, imperiling the universe.

More concrete plans include some changes in the series' sets. "We're going to put another walkway on the Promenade which will make it a little easier to shoot and block actors," said Rick Berman. "We're going to wild walls so that walls that now exist in a stationary fashion can be easily moved. It's a question of learning and fixing the things that have gone wrong in the first season."

However, the foremost philosophy which guided the first season will continue in its second, meaning that the most important exploration on the show won't be interstellar, but interpersonal. "There's been great diversity this year," said Peter Fields. "We've had a chance to explore the characters as much as I thought we could and find facets of them that I really think portend great interest for the future. It occurred to me recently that we have no idea how and when Odo came to the station as the security officer or anything else, and I said why not do a story that encompasses that? Slowly we flesh out our characters, both for the audience and for ourselves. That is much more interesting than writing the same cops and robbers show every week."

"I would like to see different combinations of characters than we've seen so far this season," said Robert Wolfe. "I think we've explored Odo and Quark, Sisko and Kira, Sisko and Dax and O'Brien and Bashir very well. I'd like to see some different combinations. Maybe see Sisko and Quark, Odo and Bashir, Kira and Dax. I think we're also going to do some more of the political intrigue."

Ira Behr, who had come off the turmoil of THE NEXT GENERATION's tumultuous third season, was surprised about how pleasant his freshman year on DEEP SPACE NINE turned out to be. "The show has been very well-received," said Behr. "I've enjoyed writing for it more than I thought I would. Michael, Rick and I have been getting along very well and I feel comfortable with them. Peter and I work well together and I just want to have some more fun with some of the characters. I think we've explored them to an extent. We can continue to do that, although the thought of 26 episodes fills me with fear and loathing on Melrose Avenue. The problem with this year being so enjoyable is it puts pressure on next year to either atone for this or be better."

"Knowing that we have to 26 episodes next year is the most angst I've ever had," said Peter Allan Fields. "I don't know how we actually did 18 episodes, but we did. There have been plenty of late nights, but not as many as other shows I can name. The atmosphere here is different than any I've ever worked in. There are shows I've worked in where there's been much more of a family feeling and everybody has laughed and giggled together and not gotten much done. On this show everyone is very pleasant and in terms of the caliber and the humor and the grace of the

people, I've been very fortunate. Maybe as this staff grows we'll get some real assholes in here, though I hope not. I don't think they'd last."

Ultimately, whether you're a fan of the new series or not, Rick Berman and Michael Piller conclusively proved that STAR TREK has a long and interesting life ahead of it — even after Gene Roddenberry's death — carrying on a tradition which began over 25 years ago, and by all indications it will continue for at least another 25 more. "Rick and I had a vision that was the outgrowth of Gene Rodden-berry's vision, and we have stayed very true to his ideals in this new show," said Piller. "We have expanded the universe and put on a successful television show, and not many people in this life get a chance to do that. It's been very rewarding and it ain't done yet, but it's an awfully good beginning."

As the series prepares to enter its second year, Shimerman has several hopes for his character's continuing development. "I would like to see Quark become a little bit less blatant. I would like his intentions, his desires, to be somewhat more obscure. That would make it a little bit easier to play and I think that's what the audience is now expecting. If they keep getting the same sort of obvious things over and over, they'll know who I am and there will be no excitement. There will be no interest. There will be no desire to see what will he do next, because you pretty much know. I'll be telegraphing what I'll be doing. So I would

like to see him become a little bit more devious and it would be great if in one episode, like in 'Babel', Quark would get to save the day once or twice."

Using the CASABLANCA analogy, which has been used so frequently in describing the series, Shimerman responded to whether he views his character more like Humphrey Bogart or Sidney Greenstreet in that classic film. "Well, I have the teeth, so I must be Humphrey Bogart," he laughed. "I certainly run the casino, so I'm definitely the Humphrey Bogart of Deep Space Nine."

In DEEP SPACE NINE's second year, the crew of the station will continue exploring brave new worlds beyond the wormhole and exploring the fascinating nuances of character which have already endeared the ensemble to a new generation of STAR TREK fans. The season begins with a three-part episode followed by several intriguing new dilemmas for its crew, including Quark's encounter with a female Ferengi, Dax's symbiont being stolen and the Cardassians' villainous machinations in attempting to doom the Federation/Bajoran alliance. Even as the Vedek's vie for power in the Kai's absence, the Gamma quadrant will continue to figure prominently in the adventures that lay ahead for the gallant crew of Deep Space nine.

"I'm pleased to see the spirituality coming back," said Morgan Gendel. "The political thriller works better on DEEP SPACE NINE than on NEXT GENERATION, and when you see that little minx, Kira, in that

Even at a "Star Trek" convention, Armin Shimerman (Quark) isn't safe from the Klingons (photo copyright ©1994 Karen Witkowski)

little outfit trying to seduce a Cardassian and being tortured, it's neat stuff which broadens the range of what we see. The whole Machiavellian behind-the-scenes thing I also love.

"On the other hand, they can do this real spiritual stuff. We had a taste of it with her confronting the orb and I'd like to continue to see it go in that direction as the underpinning for some kind of action."

SEASON ONE
EPISODE GUIDE

"Emissary"

"Past Prologue"

"A Man Alone"

"Babel"

"Captive Pursuit"

"Q-Less"

"Dax"

"The Passenger"

"Move Along Home"

"The Nagus"

"Vortex"

"Battle Lines"

"The Storyteller"

"Progress"

"If Wishes Were Horses"

"The Forsaken"

"Dramatis Personae"

"Duet"

"In the Hands of the Prophets"

The extraordinary novel, based on the blockbuster pilot episode for the exciting new television series!

#1

STAR TREK

DEEP SPACE NINE

EMISSARY

POCKET
BOOKS

Episode #1
"Emissary"

Original Airdate: 1/4/93
Story by Rick Berman and Michael Piller
Teleplay by Michael Piller
Directed by David Carson

Guest Starring:
Patrick Stewart (Captain Jean Luc Picard/Locutus), Camille Saviolla (Kai Opaka), Felecia Bell (Jennifer), Marc Alaimo (Gul Dukat)

Commander Benjamin Sisko is placed in command of the Deep Space Nine space station, located in orbit of the planet Bajor. DS9, as it's more commonly referred to, has recently been vacated by the Cardassians' occupying forces. Upon his arrival, Sisko's new command team is only first being assembled when he learns that the mystical prophet of Bajor, Kai Opaka, has the last in a series of mysterious orbs, all believed to have been confiscated by the Cardassians.

Investigating the orb, Sisko is plunged into the first known stable wormhole, wherein lies the alien prophets who fear humanity and cannot understand the nature of linear existence. While Sisko professes the basic goodness of humanity, Major Kira Nerys and the rest of DS9 are placed in a battle situation with a Cardassian warship.

◻◻◻◻◻

The creation of the series' two-hour premiere was the single most difficult undertaking of DEEP SPACE NINE's first year. The telefilm's budget is estimated at over $12 million, a staggering sum for the medium.

The pilot, which tells the story of Commander Benjamin Sisko's assignment to the station along with the introduction of its key personnel, began shooting on August 18th 1992 without most of its lead actors even being cast, and principal photography was completed on September 18, 1992.

David Carson said of the extensive preparation for the show, "I'm one of those people who believes preparation is an immensely important thing. You can save time and money by preparing properly and you can also examine everything from all the angles with all the possibilities that have to be thought about. You can then produce a product that is far superior to one that is shot from the hip, on the run as it were. Although you may be very fortitious when you shoot form the hip because it's very exciting, and it does get the adrenaline going, I'm one of those people who tends to think that overall planning is one of the most important ele-ments. If you have the time to plan properly and carefully put together a jigsaw that tells a story, you'll have a much more effective result in the end."

But even with Piller's teleplay completed weeks before production began, shooting the pilot was an incredibly arduous affair complicated by delays in casting and set construction which made it — arguably — an even more difficult shoot than 'Encounter At Farpoint' six years earlier. "I had the same anxieties and hesitations about even wanting to do it because I knew what a struggle it was going to be, and the pilot was hard," said producer David Livingston, a who had been hired by Robert Justman as production manager of the NEXT GENERATION two-hour opener. "It was hard. Fortunately I didn't have to deal with the day to day minutia of a production manager and I could sort of sit back a little bit. Bob DellaSantina, the wonderful production manager I hired to do this job, just took care of everything for me. It was tough and I told everyone it was going to be tough. It wasn't like just doing another episode or a double episode. It's doing a whole new thing again. It was a pilot and we had all forgotten what that was like. We've had the Life of Riley here for five years and it's all going to change I said — and that was true. It was very difficult because there so many dynamics working; building all these new sets and a whole new cast and new wardrobe. Michael Westmore had to create a bunch of new make-ups, including Odo's, which was very difficult. All of those dynamics made it very, very difficult."

Although most of the cast was lined up before production began, late casting of the role of Sisko as well as that of Dax, one week into shooting on the pilot, made it an extremely difficult shoot for the department heads. "They cast early, but we couldn't get them until one week before the show started shooting," said costume designed Robert Blackman. "The principals arrived pretty much at the same time, but for an episode where there was a lot for them to do and a lot of multiple costumes, it was difficult. Sisko had six or seven outfits to wear in the pilot. As we get a board with a shooting schedule saying the first week you'll be shooting this and the second you'll be shooting this and the third and so on, that's how we build, in that kind of order, since everything is made to order. We had a lot of the background costumes started but the shooting schedule started changing when they

didn't have Dax cast and the more they would pull stuff up from the fifth week of shooting and stick it into the first week, the more you're completely unprepared. It was amazing, but we pulled it off."

With most of the cast in place, the impending beginning of principal photography on August 18th made the casting search a race against the clock since it was imperative that Sisko and Dax be cast before photography actually began on the pilot.

"It's an ugly business and its interminable and it's exhausting," said Rick Berman. "We have a wonderful casting director [Junie Lowry-Johnson C.S.A.] and we just began the process. I think that Rene Auberjonois is a remarkable actor, I think Nana is remarkable and my favorite on STAR TREK since the beginning has been Colm Meaney. I adore Colm's work. Armin Shimerman who has worked with us, we brought in on Quark, having been on NEXT GENERATION three different times, and he's just an actor who I've always respected. He came in to read for Quark and just nailed it. So with Colm Meaney and Siddig [El Fadil, Dr. Bashir] and Rene and Nana Visitor and Armin we had a core of five remarkable actors and it finally came down to our star and the role of Dax,

which were the two killers."

The search for Sisko was the first one to be filled only days before production began, prompting Avery Brooks to reportedly pronounce, "This is the role of my career." Piller and Berman had even toyed with casting El Fadil as Sisko after Berman discovered him in the PBS' telefilm, A DANGEROUS MAN, and arranged to put him on tape in England. When the two producers realized the actor was only 25 years old at the time, they knew they would need to look elsewhere for the commander and finally found Avery Brooks, who in addition to touring in a play about the life of Paul Robeson, is best known as Hawk from ABC'S SPENCER FOR HIRE and the short-lived spin-off, A MAN CALLED HAWK.

"Patrick Stewart has a very big pair of shoes to fill and we needed to find someone who was different but had the same stature and the same strength and power," said Rick Berman. "It was a very, very long search. We brought people from Belgium, we brought people from England, we saw German actors, English actors, we saw a lot of American actors, black actors, white actors, Hispanic actors and we finally chose Avery Brooks who was undoubtedly the best. But it was a very, very long process."

Equally difficult was the casting of the Trill science-officer. Originally envisioned as an alien in a jet-propelled wheelchair due to a difference in the station's gravity from her home planet, Piller and Berman were ultimately both drawn to the race of Trill which existed as a joined species as first examined in NEXT GENERATION's "The Host." This was Rene Echevaria's outstanding fourth season episode in which an alien ambassador having an affair with Dr. Crusher is discovered to be an alien parasite that exists within the body of a host carrier. "Originally, we had the science officer in a wheelchair since she came from a planet with different gravity," said Piller. "Eventually Ro befriends her and finds her a gravity-free environment where she could fly. Out of her office she would be in a wheelchair to move around. Although a character like this could possibly show up in the future, production requirements made her untenable on a regular basis, so we looked at a variety of other alien species and, of them, the Trill seemed the most interesting."

The Trill of DEEP SPACE NINE now exists within the body of a 28-year-old female. Having once known Sisko in its previous body, that of an old man, created a fascinating dramatic and comic relationship between Dax and Commander Sisko.

The search for the woman who could portray the Trill was the most arduous one. When the producers finally decided on Terry Farrell [HELLRAISER III] they were already weeks into production on the pilot.

"I was stressed to death," said Farrell of being the last actor to join the cast. "They did all my stuff in one week and I had the flu and my period and 16 hour days and a big lump on my forehead that we reshot for two days."

After Paramount executives reviewed the dailies on the pilot, they issued one of their few ultimatums. The distinguishing marks on Farrell's forehead, denoting her as a Trill as actor Franc Luz had worn in "The Host" as Odan, had to go. After the protracted search for a beautiful actress who could also act, the studio didn't want her to be defaced by prosthetics. "They are different Klingons and now there are different Trills," joked Farrell. "Maybe I'm from the north of Trill and the other guy was from the South."

Because of the late casting of many of the principals, Carson was deprived of extensive rehearsal time with the actors. "One of the great weaknesses we had because our casting was left till so late, was we did not have enough time to rehearse. Normally, that doesn't matter in television because you're not dealing with things that are rehearsable, but this project was so complicated in some of its philosophical content and so difficult, that it would have benefited greatly for all of us and helped in the gradation of the characters through the scenes."

"I thought we had a very ambitious pilot," said Michael Piller, who wrote the teleplay based on a story he wrote with Rick Berman. "I think the script that I wrote attempted to do things you don't ever see on television, that's really what you have to try to do if you want to be doing interesting, creative things. We took a lot of risks and it was very ambitious and when it was all done and on film and cut together, I thought it was going to be a disaster. Rick spent week after week in the editing room recutting, trimming, patching and fixing and, ultimately, at my insistence, reshooting major sequences. The post production people worked 24 hours a day for weeks to make those things look good. When I saw it on film for the first time, I was blown away and realized it finally worked."

Among the scenes that

were reshot were several with Terry Farrell as Dax. "She had a cold," Piller recalled. "Terry, who was the hardest to cast, has managed to impress us week by week with her growth and her ability to do what is asked of her to do. That was a very hard role to find somebody who could pull it off. She's done a wonderful job."

Additional reshooting involved several scenes with Avery Brooks. "We reshot Sisko's first scene with Kira," said Piller. "We didn't reshoot the Sisko/Quark scene — although I wanted to. We also reshot part of the scene with Sisko and Jake in their quarters. They were all first hour things and the reason was I felt that Sisko was very unlikeable on first meeting, and that if we did not make him more personable we would lose the audience. I felt it was terribly important that he be a competent, respect-worthy commander even though he was troubled when he came aboard. We asked Avery to go back in with Nana and reshoot a couple of things and make a few changes that softened him, which I think helped enormously."

"One of the things that appealed to me about the script was that it was very unusual to tell a story like this," said David Carson. "Essentially, it's about a Starfleet officer who does not want to take over the command that he's told to take over. And bitterly resents the officer that is ordering him to do this to such an extent that his resentment is literally murderous, because he believes that he was directly responsible for the death of his wife. That's a pretty strong story you have there. I think it was felt by the studio that we should tilt the balance back towards more affability, certain things were taken out of the script, like looking for other jobs."

Added Carson, "Michael's stage directions emphasized that Sisko was constantly unhappy, restless, disliking the Cardassian architecture and everything that went with it. He was appalled with what was going on there, but nevertheless was there to do his job. But if you tell a story about a guy whose just there to do his job, he doesn't have that spark of get up and go, and let's solve the mystery, that you associate with a STAR TREK story. I think Michael and Rick were rightly very careful to keep the basic elements that have always been very common to STAR TREK stories and characters. It's a fascinating process of trying to make sure the facets of the character that are presented immediately to the audience are rich and yet immediately accessible and, in that sense, I think there is good in both ways of doing it."

Said Rick Berman, putting a positive spin on the changes he had the clout to order, "The stuff that we reshot is very normal on a pilot. We probably did less than most two-hour pilots. It wasn't a question of making him more sympathetic, as far as I was concerned. I think Michael and I had very specific ideas about what we wanted and the actors were just getting their feet wet."

"I was very happy to reshoot it," said director David Carson of the scenes involving the commander. "I'm one of those people who shoots the first day and the second day and then wants to do it all again because as you go along you learn more about the people you're working with and what you can do with them. The bits that we reshot showed more of a military man with a problem. When we confronted the script to start with in terms of performance, the basic premise of the script was here is this man with his son coming to take over a space station where he doesn't want to be and an appointment which he resents. At that time, there were clear indications that he was being offered a job back at a university on earth and he was sounding like he was going to take it. He would have done anything to get off the station. He also hated Picard for what he perceived he did to his wife. When you take those elements together and you set off to tell a story about a man who is basically your hero and leading DS9 into other worlds and galaxies for what you hope will be a long series, it's very difficult to find the balance in performance between angst and unhappiness and yet project a personality that your audience would want to let into their living room everytime he comes on the screen. It's a very fine line to draw."

Over twenty minutes of footage was cut from the two-hour broadcast of "Emissary," scenes which may be restored by Paramount on a forthcoming video release. "I miss it all," said Berman. "There's a wonderful scene where Sisko goes back down to Bajor to return the orb to Kai Opaka that we took out. Cutting is horrible, especially when it's something so close to you as the pilot was."

"When you shoot a lot of stuff and commit yourself to doing it, you do miss the bits and pieces that are inevitably lost when you have to get it down to time," said David Carson. "I think there are sections of it I would like to see back. When you try and bring it down to time, everybody loses something they like. In the end you have to separate yourself from your own wishes

and go with what's good for the project. There are details of storytelling I liked having in there. I always liked the balance of the teaser at a slightly longer length with some more details of exactly how Sisko finds everybody during the Borg attack and where they all are. As far as television is concerned, the special effects people did such a wonderful job that its excitement was well sustainable for longer."

Because of the conceptually challenging nature of the teleplay, the myriad script changes made the shooting more difficult. "I think one of the reasons is that you're dealing with complex subjects," he said. "It isn't like doing MARRIED WITH CHILDREN. You don't actually know what subject matter you're dealing with as you're going along. The number of checks and balances a script has to go through are very great. When I arrived to do 'Yesterday's Enterprise,' it was nothing more than an outline to prepare with. It makes things very difficult when the scripts aren't ready. At the same time, I never think it's good idea to have the scripts ready if they're not very good. I've always thought that it doesn't matter when the script arrives, provided that it's bloody good when it gets there. If you sort of settle for it, six days in advance,

because you've got to make a schedule and it isn't that good and you can do it on time and on budget, I don't think you're really winning the game."

"Every time I see the show, I start to cry," admitted Terry Farrell. "I must have watched it at least six times. Sisko loves Jake and his wife so much — and everybody understands what it's like to live a little bit too much in your past and to live with the death of someone you love that much. How to figure out how to live without them is very scary."

"I think we were all happily surprised at the response," said Rick Berman of the universal acclaim that greeted the series premiere. "I knew that we had created a show that had wonderful potential and, slowly but surely, I knew that it was coming together and was going to be wonderful. I expected it would be successful, but I didn't expect it would be as successful as it was and I was a little bit amazed. We were in TIME and NEWSWEEK and the ratings have been really good. I think that both Michael and I are the kind of people who aren't all that comfortable with praise. As a result we just sort of brush it aside and plunge on, which is what we've been doing."

Said Supervising Producer David Livingston, "We were just flabbergasted. When I went to the screening here on the lot, I hadn't seen it with all the music and effects and opticals, and I was blown away by it. To know the audience responded the way they did was very gratifying. Rick's and Michael's vision, and then David Carson's execution and the wonderful cast we picked, all clicked. It's great to know you can strike gold twice now."

ALTMAN (* 1/2)** "Emissary", the DEEP SPACE NINE telefilm, which brings Commander Benjamin Sisko to Deep Space Nine to administrate the Bajoran space station vacated by the Cardassians, is far more dramatically compelling than the comparatively ponderous "Encounter At Farpoint" launch of NEXT GENERATION, but while devoid of solar starfish has problems of its own.

Substituting top heavy mystical New Age mumbo jumbo for the familiar scientific Trek-ian technobabble, Piller aims for the cerebral resonance of the best moments of "The Cage", but "Emissary" is not always a success in that regard. Its first hour is top notch TREK, establishing the premise of the new series and introducing the intriguing array of new characters sparked by a powerful and enticing teaser. However, the

film's second hour is considerably less involving as it grows mired in Sisko's metaphysical journey into his "pagh". The opener suffers from the same problems that plagued "Farpoint" with an impressive first hour and disappointing second half. DEEP SPACE works best while exploring the decks of DS9 and secular humanism and becomes muddled once Sisko begins his mystical, religious journey.

Despite a few missteps, the outstanding quality of the production values on every level are undeniable with the exception of a disappointing new main title sequence and theme. Kudos to Michael Piller who manages to translate his affinity for baseball into the ingenious means for explaining linear existence to the befuddled aliens inhabiting the wormhole.

GROSS (*1/2):** Now *that's* a pilot. Whereas NEXT GEN's "Encounter at Farpoint" was a premiere that clearly demonstrated the somewhat desperate attempts of its creators to somehow match the success of the original incarnation, DEEP SPACE NINE effortlessly (almost too much so) manages to establish its own distinct identity as a part of — yet apart from — what we've seen before. Perhaps the best analogy would be the James Bond

film series. When Sean Connery finally retired his license to kill, there was a great deal made about the fact that Roger Moore was taking over the role. Could he do it? How would he compare? Needless to say, Moore molded Bond into his own image and had an extremely successful seven-film run before being replaced by Timothy Dalton. Audiences and critics seemed to embrace Dalton much easier than they had his predecessor. This is akin to NEXT GEN, which had the entire STAR TREK legend to live up to. Ultimately, though, it did live up to its own history, perhaps in the minds of some even surpassing its progenitor series. Insofar as DEEP SPACE NINE is concerned, it had been done once already, so the second time was much easier. Now, with the third series (STAR TREK: VOYAGER) coming in January '95, one would imagine it, too, will be as easily accepted as DS9.

The Michael Piller/Rick Berman storyline immediately draws you in to this new TREK environment, and as each subsequent character is introduced, we are given very distinct examples of the conflict that exists between them. Aided by David Carson's direction, we as an audience get the same sense of disorientation that greets the characters as they come to grips with how their lives are changing.

A real highlight comes in the early scene between Sisko and Picard, which is alive with tension. When Sisko makes mention of the fact that his wife was killed at Warf 359, the implication is immediate. Yet Picard offers no apologies and doesn't even address the issue, although the nuances of Patrick Stewart's facial expression reveals much about the character's guilt as he relives the entire Locutus/Borg affair in a split second.

All in all, with "Emissary" they were off to a hell of a start.

Episode #2
"Past Prologue"

Original Airdate: 1/18/93
Written by Katharyn Powers
Directed by Winrich Kolbe

Guest Starring:
Jeffrey Nordling (Tahna), Andrew Robinson (Garak), Barbara March (Lursa), Vaughn Armstrong (Gul Dunar), Richard Ryder (Bajoran Deputy), Susan Bay (Admiral), Gwynyth Walsh (B'Etor)

Kira is reunited with former underground rebel Tahna, who comes to DS9 claiming that his days of violence are over. At the same time, Dr. Bashir meets with Cardassian tailor Garek, who is also a

Nana Visitor as Major Kira Nerys (photo copyright ©1994 Gamma Liaison)

rumored spy. Together they uncover a plot involving the Klingon sisters Lursa and B'Etor, who are delivering an explosive device to Tahna. The former resistance fighter, it turns out, plans on using the bomb to close up the wormhole and remove Bajor from the influence of both the Federation and the Cardassians.

ㅁㅁㅁㅁㅁ

Katharyn Powers, who also wrote NEXT GENERATION's "Code of Honor" recalled, "As filmed, the story was, structurally, very close to my original conception. One significant difference is that Tahna and Kira had once been lovers, but Michael decided that that was too cliched. Also in my original story, Tahna planned to continue his terrorist activities, but he changed at the end after Kira convinced him that he should work for peace. Then he was assassinated by his own people. It would be like somebody from the IRA deciding that they were going to work for the British government and try and make peace between Ireland and Britain."

"We didn't want your typical Cardassian in there," said director Winrich Kolbe. "Obviously, it would have been hard to put a real Cardassian soldier in a clothing store. Perhaps it would have been terrific, who knows, but what we felt we had to deal with was somebody abnormal — at least as far as the Cardassians were concerned. It was one of those things where I wasn't quite sure whether Andy Robinson would be the right guy. I had a different idea as to what type of actor I wanted, but Andy Robinson was available and turned out to be terrific. To me, what I wanted, which shows how far off I was, was Sidney Greenstreet. I have to admire an actor who has to come in at three in the morning and stay in that kind of make-up for the rest of the day and still be able to give a performance."

"The next time Bashir meets Garak, they'll get on better," said actor Siddig El Fadil. "He's not going to be so freaked out by the fact that he's a spy. He'll still be a little tentative about the fact he's a Cardassian however."

ALTMAN (** 1/2): Major Kira must confront her divided loyalties between her past as a

Bajoran terrorist and her duties as the Federation liaison aboard DS9 in this fairly routine first one-hour episode which, at least, is light years beyond TNG's "The Naked Now".

Certainly indicative of the show's more passionate approach to character interaction is a terrific scene between Odo and Kira, and Sisko's rejoinder to Kira after she disputes Sisko's actions with a Starfleet Admiral.

The real standout here is the relationship between a Cardassian spy, Garak, played by an effete Andy Robinson [HELLRAISER and DIRTY HARRY] and Siddig El Fadil as Bashir, who brings a manic enthusiasm to his role. It instills the episode with a vibrancy that's lacking in the espionage story although Lursa and Bator (and their wonderful Bob Blackman designed costumes) are welcome additions.

GROSS (**1/2): Although falling short of "Emissary," "Past Prologue" is a fairly strong episode that continues to establish conflict between the characters, particularly between Sisko and Kira when she goes over his head to Starfleet after deciding that she doesn't like his handling of the situation. When Sisko tells her that if she goes over his head again, he'll have hers on a serving platter, you believe it.

The political aspect of the storyline — a warrior refusing to end his struggle and willing to kill anyone in the name of his cause — is effective, and initiates the development of Kira's character from a Bajoran freedom fighter to someone who has to begin living by the rules. Andrew Robinson has a great time as Cardassian tailor Garak, but Siddig El Fadil is really annoying as a completely naive Bashir.

Episode #3
"A Man Alone"

Original Airdate: 1/18/93
Story by Gerald Sanford
& Michael Piller
Teleplay by Michael Piller
Directed by Paul Lynch

Guest Starring:
Rosalind Chao (Keiko), Edward Laurance Albert (Zayra), Max Grodenchik (Rom), Peter Vogt (Bajoran Man #1), Aron Eisenberg (Nog), Stephen James Carver (Ibudan), Yom Klunts (Old Man/Ibudan)

Shortly after having a confrontation with Odo, a Bajoran (Ibudan) once arrested by the constable for murder, turns up dead and all eyes turn to Odo. While Odo attempts to overcome these suspicions and a tide of racism rising around him, Bashir discovers DNA samples in Ibudan's quarters which may reveal the identity of the true murderer.

At the same time, Keiko O'Brien attempts to launch a school for the children of DS9, and a friendship is forged between Jake Sisko and the Ferengi youth, Nog.

ᵔᵔᵔᵔᵔ

In explaining the original story premise that he pitched to the DS9 staff, writer Gerald Sanford said, "I thought it might be an interesting show to have someone accuse Odo of being a Nazi of the Cardassians who had murdered people. He's accused of this, although we find out later it's not true. So what I wanted to do was a story about what one's false accusations could lead to. Michael liked the idea and we developed it. The more we talked about it, the more we came to a point where someone did accuse him of murder. Then we came up with the notion of using the holosuite where a client is killed and Odo is the only one who could have gotten in and gotten out. People blame him for it, and how does he get out of it? In my original version, the only one who believed Odo was innocent was Sisko, but even he starts to believe it. He has to really go out on a limb and finally there's so much evidence that goes against Odo that he, too, has to believe it. Even his own

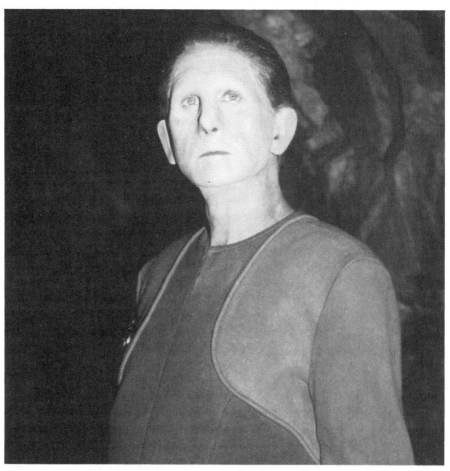

Rene Auberjonois as the shape-shifting head of security, Odo (photo copyright © 1994 Gamma Liaison)

crew began to say, 'Hey, when you're caught up in the regime, you begin acting like the regime.' I really did want to do say something but it was totally changed around.

"When I first came on the show," Sanford elaborated, "they had sold it but I was one of the first writers they hired and they were trying to figure out how the show should develop. I came in with seven or eight ideas and they liked three or four. Then they said, 'Gee, maybe we ought to do a sort of GRAND HOTEL style in

this particular episode and do a lot of vignettes all taking place around the station. I did one treatment the old way, using about two basic stories, and then Michael Piller said, 'Let's pick three more of these stories and make it really like GRAND HOTEL, a lot of things going on at once.' So I wrote the story up with about five of the vignettes and really never heard from them again."

Said Supervising Producer Ira Steven Behr, "I always thought the ending was weak with the Mission:

Impossible-like taking off of the mask. There are things I find weak about some of these shows that have nothing to do with the writing. I felt that show was hurt by the pacing. Many of the shows at the beginning of the season lacked pacing. I liked what we tried to do with the character of Zayra, which is show a character that would be a problem for us to face on a semi-recurring basis. That never really worked out. Plus we never brought him back either."

"'A Man Alone' is a very soft episode and a soft character show with some serious conflicts in it, and it's a wonderful show that defines our characters in ways they weren't in the pilot," said Michael Piller. "It was felt it was too soft to be the first hour, so we decided that 'Past Prologue' would be more appropriate to follow the two-hour since it had a better action quotient and was a real opportunity for us to continue the themes that had been set up in the pilot and to see what happens when a terrorist comes onboard. Oddly enough, I thought that in post the addition of music and effects lifted 'Man Alone' where they didn't really help 'Past Prologue' much."

"It was the first chance to see Armin and Rene work together as a wonderful team

and it was quite a compelling story," said director Paul Lynch. "It was the first show we shot so they were a little more relaxed about schedule and as the show went on, they tightened up. It gave one a chance to explore what the DEEP SPACE NINE series was about."

ALTMAN (**): In the series' requisite murder mystery, usually reserved as the fodder for fueling the engines of a creatively bankrupt series during its waning seasons, "A Man Alone" involves Odo being accused of killing a freed convict who he sent to prison years before. CAPE FEAR, it's not and it's easy to understand why the first episode filmed was switched with the second ("Past Prologue").

What works within the familiar trappings are the inspired character moments, particularly between Dax and Bashir and the developing Odo and Quark relationship. Not all together unpalatable is the B-story in which Keiko establishes a school aboard the ship. What doesn't work at all is the story's soapbox preaching regarding tolerance in which a contrived scene of mob violence takes place in front of Odo's office. There's no dramatic justification for the violence and so Sisko's chiding has little resonance. Also, the plot's denemaux

involving cloning which is not entirely unexpected, but completely hokey.

GROSS (**1/2): And the conflict continues as Odo's sensibilities come up against Sisko's, and the question of how far one can go to enforce a personal set of laws is raised. Subplot wise, the series continues to lay down the groundwork for the characters, including the establishing of friendship between Jake Sisko and Nog, and the fascinating Trill/host relationship between Dax and Sisko. Bashir, however, in his attempts to pick up Dax is *really* annoying. Keiko is given a nice turn as she attempts to find a purpose for herself and locks on to teaching.

The biggest problem with the murder mystery is that you don't believe for a second that Odo is guilty. When a similar situation was raised regarding Scotty on the original series episode "Wolf in the Fold," they went a long way to raise the *possibility* that he was guilty.

An interesting moment is when the crowd tries to corner Odo and kill him, giving the impression of a 24th century version of *Frankenstein*. The only thing these "villagers" are missing are their burning torches.

The twist — a man killing his clone — is wonderful.

Episode #4
"Babel"

Original Airdate: 1/25/93
Story by Sally Caves
and Ira Steven Behr
Teleplay by
Michael McGreevey
and Naren Shankar
Directed by Paul Lynch

Guest Starring:
Jack Kehler (Jaheel), Matthew Falson (Surmak Ren), Ann Gillespie (Nurse Jabara), Geraldine Farrell (Balis Blin), Bo Zenga (Asoth), Richard Ryder (Bajoran Deputy), Frank Novak (Businessman), Kathleen Wirt (Aphasia Victim), Lee Brooks (Aphasia Victim), Todd Feder (Federation Male)

A Bajoran weapon designed to be utilized against the Cardassians when they occupied the space station is accidentally triggered. The result is a disease that sweeps through the station, rapidly infecting the crew by making them speak and think gibberish. Before it's too late, Kira must find the Bajoran scientist who helped develop the weapon eighteen years earlier, and retrieve the cure.

ooooo

"We had this premise for over five years at NEXT GENERATION," said Michael Piller. "It was written by the same person who wrote 'Hollow Pursuits' for us and

we had always been attracted to the idea that you could suddenly lose the ability to use language to communicate, and how people are able to communicate with each other. It's a new series and you're desperate for stories so we gave it a whirl. We used the virus as a macguffin. It wasn't a great episode but had some wonderful moments in it."

"It was a rewrite I did after having written 'Quality of Life' for NEXT GENERATION," said the show's science advisor and TNG staff writer, Naren Shankar. "It was a little rough and I had trouble believing in it initially. In some ways it's kind of a cool idea but what ultimately was never communicated was the sense of panic and helplessness which would accompany this sort of virus. You never saw people freaking out, which is what I think you would see a lot of if you suddenly thought nobody in the world could understand you. I know I would get upset. It just didn't come across and you just walk through an empty station of quiet people instead of a rioting station of screaming people with flames coming out of things and people just going bananas. Obviously, from a production standpoint you can't do that, but it was unfortunate. It was a high concept show and you always run the risk that when you go to write

it down there's not as much there as you think there might be. I liked the teaser and the ending where we broke the ship away from the docking ring before it exploded."

"The inability to communicate was fun but I don't think it went far enough," said Ira Behr. "It became 'let's see who's going to get aphasia next' and I thought that was a bit of a problem. Sisko's scenes with the kid were nice and the scenes with O'Brien were well done, although the pacing in the teaser was lethargic."

As for the meaning of Babel's aphasiac babbling, Behr smiled, "That's for the scholars," he offered, wryly noting that the actors were not allowed to improvise it on the set. "I don't think computers are powerful enough to pick out the secret messages that are in 'Babel.' We did not want the music of 'Babel' to be tampered with because when you do that on the set, there's a chance that by mistake you get some coherency in it and we wanted it to lack even a hint of coherency — nor did we want anyone to tamper with the secret of the universe contained within that dialogue."

ALTMAN (**): The old reliable STAR TREK chestnut in which a virus imperils the crew of DEEP SPACE is resurrected unsuccessfully. By now, watching the station functioning poorly is becoming tired and the cliched virus story is similarly unengaging with an all-too quick wrap-up in which an antidote is found and administered during the commercial break. The only element that keeps the story interesting is the always lively banter between Quark and Odo. Shimerman has quickly distinguished himself as one of the ensemble's most interesting actors, endowing his character of Quark with a perverse sense of twisted, greedy nobility.

GROSS (**): Some humorous Odo/Quark moments as well as O'Brien's attempts to hold the station together just aren't enough to overcome the weaknesses of this episode. STAR TREK seems to have created a genre upon itself in the disease of the week category. In this case, the disease was clearly inspired by an episode of THE NEW TWILIGHT ZONE, in which Robert Klein was offered dinosaur instead of breakfast by his wife, who, like the rest of the world, seemed to be speaking gibberish to him. So while the notion of the disease is interesting in that it had been created as a Bajoran weapon against the Cardassians, the cure — in which Kira finds someone involved in its development 18 years earlier — stretches credi-

Colm Meaney as Chief O'Brien made the leap from "Next Generation" to ""DS9" (photo copyright ©1994 Gamma Liaison)

bility to the next star system.

Episode #5
"Captive Pursuit"

Original Airdate: 2/1/93
Story by Jill Sherman Donner
Teleplay by Jill Sherman Donner and Michael Piller
Directed by Corey Allen

Guest Starring:
Scott MacDonald (Tosk),
Gerrit Graham (The Hunter),
Kelly Curtis (Miss Sarda)

O'Brien uses a DS9 tractor beam to pull in a dam-

aged vessel piloted by a reptilian alien who identifies himself only as Tosk. After an uneasy beginning, O'Brien and Tosk establish something of respect and friendship for each other. Things grow darker, however, when a group of armed aliens arrive on DS9, determined to capture Tosk.

Tosk, O'Brien and everyone else is surprised to note, accepts his fate easily, with the truth soon being revealed: Tosk and all of his people have been created specifically to be hunted as sport, and their role in society is considered an honorable one. Recognizing the reality of the situation, O'Brien pulls a few mechanical strings that allow the hunt to continue.

¤¤¤¤¤

"One of my favorite episodes of the season," said Michael Piller. "The real problem was to make it credible and that's what I had to address in my rewrite. The relationship had to be strong enough that O'Brien would bond to this character enough to go against his Starfleet responsibilities."

Scott MacDonald who played Tosk returned on THE NEXT GENERATION to play N'vek in sixth season's "Face of the Enemy." "'Captive Pursuit' was my favorite show of the first half dozen for all the obvious reasons," said Rick Berman. "Everything worked out well and the character of Tosk was a creature who was immediately both fascinating and sympathetic. The relationship that developed between he and O'Brien was charming."

Commented Ira Behr, "It was a good show for O'Brien and it was a good show all the way down the line with the guy running around in the goddamned lizard suit. I immediately have that against it, but the whole point, from the very beginning, was we were in love with the idea of

someone coming through the wormhole after this creature that they had basically bred for this hunt, and he lives at a level that we usually don't live on. We live on a much duller, plodding level of life experience. The fact that O'Brien gets involved with him, I thought created a nice relationship. The whole episode was very well done."

ALTMAN (***): DEEP SPACE finally begins fulfilling its early promise in this engaging action/adventure in an intergalactic "most dangerous game." Although Corey Allen's direction is somewhat lackluster and the station continues to feel claustrophobic, it's the first opportunity for O'Brien to really shine and Colm Meaney is well up to the challenge. The requisite phaser fights aren't all that well executed, leaving it to the dramatic confrontation between Sisko and O'Brien to serve as the primary source of incinderary conflict in the episode's more than satisfying coda.

GROSS (*1/2):** At last, all of the elements of DS9 come together in this fascinating fox-on-the-run tale, with a twist (that the "fox" has been created specifically to serve as the hunted) that would make Rod Serling proud.

Sure there are phaser

battles and some effective suspense in the course of the hunt on DS9, but the core of the episode is the wonderful relationship between O'Brien and Tosk. By the time the hour is up, it is completely believable that these two characters have gone from members of two race encountering each other for the first time to genuine friends. Real kudos to Colm Meaney and Scott MacDonald for pulling it all off.

Episode #6
"Q-Less"

Original Airdate: 2/8/93
Story by
Hannah Louise Shearer
Teleplay by
Robert Hewitt Wolfe
Directed by Paul Lynch

Guest Starring:
John DeLancie (Q), Jennifer Hetrick (Vash), Van Epperson (Bajoran Clerk), Laura Cameron (Bajoran Woman), Tom McCleister (Kolos)

Vash, an archeologist first introduced in an episode of STAR TREK: THE NEXT GENERATION, is found in the Gamma Quadrant by a DS9 runabout. Sisko is curious about how she got there, but Vash is not talking, merely expressing her interest in having Quark auction off artifacts discovered on her adventure.

Shortly thereafter,

though, Q appears, determined to convince Vash to rejoin him in their exploration of the cosmos. She refuses and, partly in anger, Q takes it out on the DS9 crew, taunting Sisko in particular. While all of this is going on, the station begins to lose power. Everyone suspects Q is playing more of his games, but he insists that he's innocent while simultaneously refusing to help. Ultimately it is discovered that one of Vash's artifacts is actually an alien creature that has been absorbing energy from the station.

ロロロロロ

Q's most recent appearance on the final frontier was in DEEP SPACE NINE's "Q-less," where he encounters Commander Benjamin Sisko for the first time unleashing his acerbic wit on the unsuspecting crew of the space station. "It was a Vash episode to begin with," said Michael Piller. "We go in and find Vash and bring her back and we were struggling to find some focus for it. I said, 'If you're going to make it Vash, why not bring Q along?', because it's the natural way to get Q onto DS9. We wanted to do a Q show and yet we were very serious about doing it in a credible way. If you just have him come on and say 'Look, is this the new show?' it's silly, but this seemed to be a justifiable way. It gave us an

John DeLancie visited DS9 and picked on "Benjy" Sisko rather than Picard in "Q-Less" (photo copyright ©1994 Karen Witkowski)

opportunity to have Q play some games with some of the new characters and to see how Sisko would react. It was fun."

Staff writer Robert Wolfe wrote the teleplay based on an idea by Hannah Louise Shearer (which hadn't involved Q) in which they found an archeologist in the Gamma Quadrant with an artifact that turned out to be an egg. "They invited me in to pitch DS9 and I pitched a variety of things, none of which really went anywhere," admitted Wolfe. "One of my ideas had some

small parallels to the basic story they had for 'Q-Less' and then they hired me to write that episode. There was already a story, but Q wasn't in it so I put Q into it and then wrote the teleplay. It was a Vash story and they decided they wanted to put Q into it. Q's a lot of fun to write in general. It was helpful in a way because when I pitched the stories they couldn't tell me who was playing the various parts. When I was just starting to write the episode they were just beginning to shoot the pilot. I hadn't seen anybody, which was difficult, so it was kind of nice to have some familiar characters to work with and it was fun to explore the new characters through familiar faces."

Wolfe had pitched a Q story to THE NEXT GENERATION once that hadn't been bought in which Q turned Picard, Data and Troi into officers on a Romulan ship. "The reason it didn't go is the way I had them do it: there was no Romulan make-up involved, they weren't possessing the bodies. The visual gag was the same as QUANTUM LEAP, where we would look at them and see them as themselves and maybe in a reverse shot we might see them as other people completely, but they didn't want to step on QUANTUM LEAP's toes."

Armin Shimerman, who plays Quark, joked that when the veteran TREK-ker DeLancie showed up on the sets he projected the attitude that he was the star and the cast were the guest stars. "I love that Armin quote," smiled DeLancie. "I think that one of the things I had to be careful about is I couldn't be so chameleon like as to be a different character just because I was on a different set. I had to carry on in the way that I know works for NEXT GENERATION and carry it into the new show so it

would be seamless in a way. There would be kind of a bigness about Q that maybe permeates the tide pool."

"It was interesting to watch the two of them together," said Armin Shimerman of watching Avery Brooks and DeLancie's characters' verbal jousts and literal fisticuffs in a Q-created bout of pugilism. "It was an interesting dynamic because Avery is the lead and so he has the responsibility and that recognition in himself. Yet John DeLancie came on the set with his own agenda, which is that he has played Q quite often and is very familiar with his end and thought of us sort of as the new kids. We were the regulars, he was the guest star, but he felt like he was the regular and we were the visitors."

In many ways, John DeLancie seems to be the literal personification of Q, but that's a result of his success in making the transformation into the character seem so effortless. Said the actor, "I always say the words as written, but if there were 20 people who all had to come up to play the same scenes, there would be 20 different interpretations of it. Do I put myself into the character? Yes. Is the character me? Who knows? It's a melding and that's the point of acting."

"It was only their fifth episode so it was a little differ-

ent than working on NEXT GENERATION in terms of working with new people," said Jennifer Hetrick who returned to play Vash. "The environment was also very different in terms of the whole storyline where you have many more different aliens and characters. It was very colorful and I kind of think of Quark's as the STAR WARS cantina. The characters are also a lot of fun and I liked working with John again and continuing the relationship between those two characters."

"She and I have worked a couple of times together other than STAR TREK," said John DeLancie, who last worked with the actress on ABC's THE YOUNG RIDERS. "We just spent a lot of time together trying to get our lines down for which there were a lot. While it was a nice show, the urgency of my involvement and the kind of motivation behind it that I'm in love wasn't explored in a substantive way, which leaves you with a thin thing to play. As a result, the style, the quips and the panache in which things are done become very important."

Director Paul Lynch commented, "That's Q's modus operandi and that's why it was fun to do. They really did get down that fast paced, fun stuff I like. There was a real push in order to do it in the time we had because comedy takes time to make it work. If the timing doesn't work exactly, it doesn't work at all and that takes take after take. We were always running against production conflicts because of that. To a degree, it's a little like MOONLIGHTING except that the reason MOONLIGHTING sometimes took between 12 and 18 days to do a one-hour episode was that the amount of time it took to work out the timing in long sustained scenes, which is what you want. You want the scene to play without cuts and that goes back to Howard Hawks where you would just play a scene right through and let the camera watch it. That's what makes it funny. That takes a lot of time to rehearse, to stage and to shoot because if you're a beat off at any given point, you have to go back and do the whole thing over again. That was a hard show, but comedy, as they say, is always the toughest thing to do."

"John DeLancie said it was the funniest and best material he's had as Q," said Ira Behr. "I worked a lot on that episode. Michael likes to give challenges out to the staff and the challenge in 'Q-less' was to write a scene which took place entirely in Vash's quarters: 'I want to take that as long as you can go. Make it as

funny as you can and keep people coming in.' I think it worked extremely well. I still have the bruises on my forehead from banging my head against the wall from the tech part of it. The line 'Picard would have solved this technobabble' was a line we wrote with great glee because at that point we hated the god-damned technobabble. At the time, I thought it was going to swamp the episode, but then Rick and Michael started cutting it all back."

ALTMAN (***): Maybe I'm just jaded, but haven't we seen this story before? A mysterious artifact that is actually a misunderstood lifeform — we're talking off the meter on the hoke scale, and there hasn't been an ending as insipid since "Encounter At Farpoint."

Fortunately, the episode's predictable climax is offset by its utterly brilliant acerbic bite involving Q and Vash. Everything about this story is delightful including Bashir's inept womanizing which is a striking contrast with the assured lascivious studliness of Kirk and Riker. Quite simply, Q has never been more scathing or outrageous (even in 'Deja Q') and his verbal jousts with Sisko are unmatched by anything since Kirk fenced with Harry Mudd in that old series that everyone

has forgotten about.

The ultimate laugh riot for me, however, was Quark's auction of "valuable" Gamma quadrant artifacts which were, in fact, valueless trinkets, which struck me as a writer's wry satire on the selling of STAR TREK in which the home shopping networks have marched a virtual procession of hucksters, including Michael Piller, before the cameras to sell wares to lobotomized fans. Every time the story cuts from Q and Vash to ops, I cringed as its routine jeopardy plot unfolded. Maybe it's time to give DeLancie his own show, STAR TREK: Q & A.

GROSS (***): When DS9 was announced, one got the immediate impression that there would be a barrage of crossovers between it and TNG that would have been as insipid as those on the old SIX MILLION DOLLAR MAN and BIONIC WOMAN series of the '70s in which part one would air on the former, part two on the latter and part three back on the former. Thankfully, as "Q-Less" demonstrates, this is just not the case.

The appearance of Vash and her presence in the Gamma Quadrant is perfectly logical, given what we know of her, and if Vash is here, then it's only logical that Q be here as well. And as good as Jennifer Hetrick is as Vash, John DeLancie is better, bringing some of the bite back to Q that he had in such TNG episodes as "Encounter at Farpoint," "Hide & Q" and "Deja Q." Whereas on the Enterprise he views the humans as playthings, on DS9 he could care less about them. He wants Vash — that's it! Which is not to say that he doesn't take the opportunity to have some fun with "Benjy." Because DeLancie is playing against Avery Brooks rather than Patrick Stewart, the entire dynamic is much different. I, for one, look forward to a reprise.

Insofar as the "B" story is concerned — forget about it! It's old, it's tired, it's boring.

Episode #7
"Dax"

Original Airdate: 2/15/93
Story by Peter Allan Fields
Teleplay by D.C. Fontana
and Peter Allan Fields
Directed by David Carson

Guest Starring:
Gregory Itzin (Tandro), Anne Haney (Judge Renora), Richard Lineback (Selin Peers), Fionnula Flanagan (Enina)

Dax is charged with the murder of General Ardelon Tando — thirty years earlier.

Sisko realizes that the charges are actually being levelled against Curzon Dax and not Jadzia, and he refuses to allow her to be taken as a guilty criminal. What follows is an extradition hearing which is convened to determine if the host body of a Trill can be held responsible for the alleged crimes of the symbiont.

Jadzia, who has all of Curzon's memories, refuses to say much of anything regarding guilt or innocense and it appears that she will be extradited, when the wife of General Tando enters the proceedings, announcing that it would have been impossible for Curzon to have murdered her husband because Curzon was in bed with her at the time.

□□□□□

A moment which strains credulity is when Odo cons Quark into turning over the bar for the extradition hearing. It's hard to believe that a station the size of DEEP SPACE NINE doesn't have a conference room. Countered Michael Piller, "We wanted to put it in the bar because it's an interesting set. We could have built a room for this to occur in, but the truth is we had shown the space station destroyed in the pilot three weeks before and there's no reason to believe there's a lot of usable space. Slowly, it's coming back on line, it was

not a production requirement."

"There isn't a big conference room," said David Livingston. "Everything is used for commerce or it has cargo bays and stuff. The bar had chairs already and wasn't a clothing shop or some other mercantile place. We never discussed building it and it looked okay. It saved us $50,000."

Said D.C. Fontana who wrote the first draft, "I participated very little. It was Peter Allan Fields' original story and I did the teleplay and he rewrote me and we split the teleplay credit. The only thing I think that is interesting is that I am now the only writer who's written for all four produced television versions of the series. That's about all I think is interesting."

"It was a delightful time working together," said Michael Piller of Fontana, whose agent had suggested her in response to queries sent out by Piller. "She had real trouble finding the Trill, as she would be the first to admit, and we had to really go back and put that into the script."

"I loved the scene with Avery," said Terry Farrell. "It was interesting working with him since neither of us talked to each other at all. Normally, we totally joke around and laugh and I run around and chase him and try to stick my finger in his nose and pinch his butt, but it was really weird shooting 'Dax'. I wasn't talking to him and he wasn't talking to me either. His character was angry and frustrated with my character. It's a rare moment when you do method acting on this show and it's fun to pull out those techniques when you can. It makes it more interesting as an actor to do. it was the first time all of us found out that much about a Trill, including myself. I learned more about my character reading that episode in November than anything else I had read."

After the enormity of the pilot, "Dax's" intimate character was quite a dramatic change for director David Carson. "I can do that too," he laughed. "My background is in the theater and I've worked with actors in many different situations. Words, performance and character interpretation are things that I think very often can carry a story by themselves. If you have a good story and it's all set in one room and you have two or three or four good actors who can interpret that story well and make it fascinating, you don't need locations or huge sets or spaceships wizzing around. You can tell the story very simply on that basis. I was very pleased to do that, I thought it was a very success-

Terry Farrell as Trill Science Officer Dax (photo copyright ©1994 Gamma Liaison)

ful show, marrying camera movement to performance and using the lighting to express the feelings of the piece. It worked very well as an intimate drama and has for the courtroom scenes. I haven't done LA LAW for nothing."

"A small episode, yet a very well done one that stands up to anything that was done this season to an extent," said Ira Behr. "It was one of Sisko's best shows. I think it showed him in a very good light. I liked the Odo stuff and I thought the ending when the

wife comes back was touching. Being a Trill must be very difficult, it must be incredibly schizophrenic. I think it's good that we play a little of that, instead of this initial Mr. Spock, total control. I don't think Trills can be totally in control of their lifestyles. It's a very difficult thing to have seven lives, seven voices, seven memories in your head to a certain extent."

ALTMAN (** 1/2): With the exception of a sentimental coda, "Dax" is nothing we

THE DEEP SPACE LOGBOOK

haven't seen explored numerous times before in STAR TREK's ever more voluminous history. The episode is marked by a number of lively guest performances, of which Anne Haney as Judge Els Renora is a standout. The Trill backstory is interesting and the courtroom jousting adeptly written.

GROSS (**1/2): "Dax" starts with a bang in the form of an action-packed teaser as Dax is captured and Bashir attempts to save her. The suspense continues right through the beginning of the first act when the abductors launch their vessel and are captured at the last possible moment by a tractor beam. Having accomplished these scenes alone, director David Carson could have called it a day.

Although the notion of one of the main characters being accused of murder has grown very tired (i.e. "Court Martial," "Wolf in the Fold," "A Matter of Perspective," "A Man Alone"), the nature of a Trill lends the idea a bit of innovation. Unfortunately, it's not enough.

Episode #8
"The Passenger"

Original Airdate: 2/22/93
Story by Morgan Gendel
**Teleplay by Morgan Gendel &
Robert Hewitt Wolfe and**

Michael Piller
Directed by Paul Lynch

Guest Starring:
Caitlin Brown (Kajada), James Lashly (George Primmin), Christopher Collins (Nog), James Harper (Vantika)

While traveling in a Runabout, Kira and Bashir pick up a distress signal of a disabled Kobliad ship. They beam over the pilot, a woman named Ty Kajada, and her passenger, a murderer named Rao Vantika. Vantika seemingly dies shortly after arriving on DS9, but he has actually managed to transfer his consciousness from his body to another, and continues to do so until he ends up in Bashir.

It is Vantika's goal to receive a large quantity of deuridium, a drug that is noted for prolonging the life of his people. It is only through the ingenuity of Dax that they are able to thwart his plan before taking off in a waiting vessel.

ooooo

Freelance writer Morgan Gendel, who wrote TNG's "Inner Light" and "Starship Mine," was one of the first freelancers to contribute a script to the first season of DEEP SPACE NINE. Gendel, a former NBC programming executive who has written for such shows as WISEGUY, HUNTER and LAW

& ORDER, made good use of his experience writing cop shows for this story which involved an escaped convict who may or may not have taken over the police officer escorting him to prison.

"I thought the idea of a cop who's chasing himself was something you could only do in a science-fiction show," said Gendel. "When I first pitched it, they said they were looking to do a Hannibal Lecter-like character and then the next pitch they would say, 'We want to make sure we're not doing that.' I pitched it to Ira and Peter and they called me back and said we want to talk about it with Michael [Piller], and he was ready to say let's give it a whirl when Ira, rightfully, brought up the problems we were going to face. Ira's great. He's so straightforward and very direct to writers and to Michael, so you really get a sense of exactly where you stand. Ira was raising these fears about the episode which I think turned out to be accurate, but I'm in there like a salesman — and I don't want to walk away without the sale. I said, 'I hear what you're saying, Ira, but I think I can explore it and make it work out in story' and I don't know if it was that enthusiasm or Michael felt sorry for me that day, but he said 'Okay, let's give a run at this' and, of course, there were problems."

One of the most dramatic changes from Gendel's pitch in the final version of the story was the fact that it was Bashir who became possessed as opposed to the female cop, with whom Bashir was originally supposed to develop a romantic attachment. "In my first outline, the bad guy's essence was in the cop and we captured her at the end of Act 4. What I did in Act 5 was have this woman Bashir's fallen for trying to convince him to let her out of jail because he's planted a bomb on the station. Act 5 was all about what does Bashir do. Does he trust his gut or his logic? His gut is telling him he's got to go, even at gunpoint, so that she can lead him to the bomb. That was the tension in Act 5 which leads up to where she changes back to Vanticus and this whole run and jump thing."

In "The Passenger," Quark becomes involved with the hijacking of a vital mineral shipment. "He is still the middleman," said Shimerman. "I say that in the episode, 'I'm just the middleman' when they ask me if I'm going with them. He's just trying to make a buck. But it was a darker Quark getting back to the Quark I think of in 'Emissary.' And that's good. Anytime that I get close to that I feel a little bit better. I feel more confident with that.

Siddig El Fadil as Dr. Bashir (photo copyright ©1994 Gamma Liaison)

Drama is always easier to play than comedy."

The implications of Quark's first truly illegal activity is never explored. It'll be interesting to see how long Quark can remain sympathetic when he engages in such blatantly criminal profiteering.

While actor Shimerman enjoys his character's malevolent streak, he admitted that sometimes it can go too far, which is a concern the writers are well aware of. "Quark has some bad friends," said staff writer Robert Wolfe. "He runs

with a bad crowd. He's not the kind of guy who would kill anybody. He's not a cold-blooded murderer, but he's certainly not the greatest guy on the face of the earth. We use him for comedy, but Armin has done a good job of showing that dangerous streak in him."

"He is suckered in over his head by his own greed," said director Paul Lynch. "He doesn't really go looking for trouble and if he had known what he was getting into he wouldn't have, but his own greed overruled him. It's a mystery and it owes a lot to the thriller conventions of Hitchcock, Murnau and DePalma."

"We had a very odd experience on the show," said Rick Berman. "Siddig made a choice of a voice to use that didn't work for us. It was too Bela Lugosi-like and we replaced his entire part with him again but we had him do it a different way. We didn't really know if it would work or not, but it was fine."

"I felt it was a very effective episode," said Michael Piller. "The guest cast gave great performances and it gave Bashir a chance to do something unique and different. It's a very spooky mystery and I liked all the misleads because just when you think you know what's going on, it turns out that you think maybe it's the security officer that's missing and then suddenly you get the final twist that it's Bashir. One of the things that's flawed in the episode is in the scene on the ship where Bashir is grabbed by the throat. You sort of get the feeling that's something happening at that moment."

"'The Passenger' was a show at the time I felt could have just as easily been Geordi," said Ira Behr, who believes the series' storylines should be specific to DS9 and not stories you could tell on the NEXT GENERATION. "I

think there's nothing wrong with the episode, I just don't have much of a feeling for it. It could have just as easily taken place on the Enterprise."

Another aspect for the show which never made it to the final script was writer Gendel's idea for a song that Quark would sing while cleaning the bar. "I had him singing a whole little ditty, like a hobbit," said Gendel. "I took a day to write this ditty about making money while he's serving people and shorting them on their drinks. I thought it was hysterical and also thought if I turned it in, they were going to laugh me out of the room. But Mike, if you're reading this and ever need a ditty, call me."

ALTMAN (1/2):** Despite its title, which makes it sound like Italian Neo-Realist cinema, "The Passenger" is, in fact, a rather tame genre piece in which a murderer plans to hijack a vital mineral shipment. When he is killed, he instead hijacks the bodies of those around him.

Although it's a tried and true concoction of science-fiction clichés, "The Passenger" wisely chooses to explore the character dynamics between Odo and a Starfleet Security Officer who the constable feels is encroaching on his turf. That part of the story works, although like much of DS9 the

conflict sometimes seem forced. What doesn't work is the episode's conclusion which is another all too familiar wrap-up in which technobabble substitutes for drama in resolving the plot. Quark and his rogues gallery of mercenaries are effective, however, even if dramatically Quark should be engaging in such clearly criminal endeavors.

GROSS (**): A nice addition (though subsequently dropped after another appearance) is a Starfleet security officer who immediately comes into conflict with Odo. However, the main plot — a killer gaining immortality by transferring his consciousness from one body to another — is interesting, but there's a certain lack of urgency to everything that takes place. "The Passenger" never really comes to life, and the technobabble-filled (and seemingly illogical) conclusion really mars things. Still, Siddig El Fadil has a great time chewing the scenery once his body is taken over.

Episode #9
"Move Along Home"

Original Airdate: 3/15/93
Story by Michael Piller
Teleplay by Frederick Rappaport and Lisa Rich & Jeanne Carrigan-Fauci
Directed by David Carson

Guest Starring:
Joel Brooks (Falow), James Lashly (Lieutenant George Primmin), Clara Bryant (Chandra)

When Quark cheats a delegation from the Gamma Quadrant — DS9's first contact with a different civilization from the other side of the wormhole — they decide to extract revenge by forcing the Ferengi to participate in a game whose code phrase is "Move along home."

Unbeknownst to Quark, this particular game could turn out to be deadly for Sisko, Kira, Bashir and Dax when they literally become pawns who face one danger after another, depending on how Quark plays the game. Gradually the group tries to work its way back to the station from the limbo they're trapped in, but Quark ultimately loses and seemingly sentences his comrades to death. Fortunately, though, as the leader of the aliens, Falow, notes, "It's only a game," and everyone is returned unharmed.

ロロロロロ

"It's a flawed episode and perhaps the most expensive show next to the pilot," said Michael Piller. "It was a very neat concept. We wanted to do a contest on NEXT GENERATION and while we were having a discussion about the

old PRISONER series on this show, the idea of making an episode with all these weird and strange things happening and 'how do I get out' seemed very appealing. Finding ways of making that come to life in an affordable setting was not easy. It was a monster show, but the idea of Quark cheating an alien species and them taking it out on Quark by putting us through these hoops I thought was terrific. It was one of our strongest concepts, but I had some problems with the casting and we couldn't afford to do extensive make-up or costumes. Essentially, we ended up having these aliens who are strange and weird guys coming through the wormhole in leisure suits with odd hair and tattoos. I still think it was one of the most entertaining episodes we have done."

Offered Rick Berman, "It was a big show that had a tremendous amount of problems. It turned out much better than I thought it would. There were a lot of Lewis Carroll elements to the whole thing which were always a little bit on the verge of being hokey for me, but when all was said and done, I was pleasantly surprised."

Laughed director David Carson, "I think this was their way of punishing English people. It was very difficult because the scope of the show

demanded a scale of building and sets which were certainly not in the budget, so therefore the corridors, which were pretty short, had to be expanded and doubled in length by clever use of backdrops and doors which were sometimes there and sometimes weren't. We shot in a very small space and tried to make it look as big as possible by using different perspectives."

Added Carson, "If you're dealing with a maze, a story where you have a maze, then the more amazing it can be, the better it is. Certainly the first versions of the script were much more interesting and exciting. But in terms of television, we managed to make it interesting enough to have the idea that you're actually playing with people's lives. It's like Shakespeare's quotation from KING LEAR where he says, 'We are as like flys unto the gods, they treat us for their sport.' It's an interesting analogy."

"It had a lot of production problems and it went through so many changes," said Ira Behr. "It was another one of those wonderful we'll shoot this on location shows and we ended up shooting it in a corridor and trying to make it look as interesting as possible. If you asked me which would I rather sit down and watch, I'd rather see an episode of THE

PRISONER, which does not mean the show was totally successful. But I agree with Michael totally that we shot high. You have to keep shooting high. Sometimes you hit and sometimes you miss and sometimes you fall in between — and to me this kind of fell in between. Would I greenlight that episode again? Absolutely."

ALTMAN (**): If not for David Carson's atmospheric direction and another sturdy performance from Armin Shimerman, "Move Along Home" would be a new low for the series whose plot seems more suited to LOST IN SPACE than DEEP SPACE. Again, more unsavory visitors from the Gamma quadrant imperil the senior staff. Although Michael Piller provides the requisite wit in the teaser along with some amusing exchanges bordering on the surreal throughout the game, the show originally called SORE LOSERS is just that: a loser bordering more on fantasy than science-fiction.

GROSS (**): The idea of using characters as living games pieces (Q's favorite pastime) is fine, but the episode falters in its presentation of the game itself. There simply isn't enough money in the budget to make the threats Sisko, Kira, Dax and Bashir endure seem

real. To make matters worse, our heroes have to play hopscotch at one point to proceed to the next level. Puhlease!

Interesting character moment: Quark's agony over having to make a decision in the playing of the game that could result in the death of his comrades. Gosh, never knew the guy had it in him.

As to first contact with life in the Gamma Quadrant.... well, let's hope the next encounter is more fulfilling.

Episode #10
"The Nagus"

Original Airdate: 3/22/93
Story by David Livingston
Teleplay by Ira Steven Behr
Directed by David Livingston

Guest Starring:
Max Grodenchik (Rom), Aron Eisenberg (Nog), Tiny Ron (Maihar-du), Lee Arenberg (Gral), Lou Wagner (Krax), Barry Gordon (Nava), Wallace Shawn (Zek)

An all-powerful Ferengi, the Royal Nagus Zek, arrives at Deep Space Nine to divvy up shares in the business opportunities awaiting them in the Gamma quadrant. Before apparently dying, he bestows his crown upon an unsuspecting Quark, who then becomes the object of several assassination attempts — including one

by his own brother. In the end, Zek turns out to be alive, merely testing his son to see if he would be worthy of being Nagus. Yet despite the trickery, Zek is intrigued by Quark and promises to return to DS9 some day.

ooooo

Zek is played by pint-sized playwright/actor Wallace Shawn, best known for his acting turns in "My Dinner With Andre" with Andre Gregory, "The Princess Bride" and, of course, as Diane Keaton's irresistible ex in Woody Allen's "Manhattan".

"He was brilliant," said David Livingston of Shawn. "It was Rick's idea to offer the part to Wally Shawn and I complimented him at the end of the show. I said, 'You are a totally fearless actor. You went for it and didn't hold anything back.' He was totally fearless and when he did his first scene he didn't even know what a Ferengi was. I kept saying 'more, more, bigger, bigger, let me tell you when it's too big.' I never told him to pull back. After he got the initial thing down, he sat on the stool at Quark's, which was the first scene we shot, and the moment he opened his mouth, the whole stage lit up and the cast was cracking up. The cast still quotes lines from the show with his inflection. Whenever someone makes a mistake on the set, we'll say, 'You failed miserably!' It was a comedy and having him and Armin together was a treat for me."

"We had a great time," agreed Shimerman. "He was a hoot. I've always been a big fan of his. I think his first day he was a little discombobulated by all the makeup but he got over that and at the end of the shoot he said he'd like to come back. At first, he asked 'How do I play this? What's a Ferengi?' and I gave him a little advice, but he didn't need it.

"The two of them were fearless," said Livingston. "Armin was concerned that he might go over the top and my comment to him was, 'You can't go over the top. These guys are Ferengis.' To have those two caliber people in these two roles wearing those big screwy makeups with the big ears and funny noses was a treat for me. It was a comedy and I like comedy."

"We had I think 17 Ferengi running around and nobody knew who each other was," said Shimerman of "The Nagus." "It was a fun and different type of STAR TREK episode, like the Tribbles episode of the original. The death threat to Quark I don't think was all that serious. We were much more interested in getting laughs than getting anybody to sit on the edge of their seat."

Armin Shimerman as the Ferengi, Quark (photo copyright ©1994 Celebrity Photo Agency)

Shimerman admitted that for a character that vacillates between broad comedy and menacing dramatics, he still needs to explore finding the proper level of his performance. "I don't think I have Quark down yet," said the actor. "I still think I have a lot to learn about him. I think that there are aspects to the character that neither the writers nor I have yet really come across and I'm the type of person who wants to keep honing the performance. When I worked in a theater, it was the same way. It's never the same performance twice. It's always trying to make it better on Friday night than it was on Thursday night. I know that the largeness of the performance works for Quark. I've got the basic colors. Now I have to find out the sort of shades and tones that will make it that much more pleasing not only for the audience, but for myself as well."

"It was David Livingston's idea and I steered him in the direction of THE GODFATHER and Ira executed as well as you possibly could," said Michael Piller of the show which was originally entitled FRIEND LIKE ME. "It's a very funny episode and Wally Shawn is something you've never seen on the NEXT GENERATION. He's certainly a character that is the most different from anything you'd find on THE NEXT GENERATION."

Said Rick Berman, "We had a tape made of the episode for Ira Behr and David Livingston where we laid in THE GODFATHER theme in the scene where Quark was made the Nagus and they come looking for favors from him. Neither David or Ira realized we were joking. They thought we were doing it for real. I loved 'The Nagus' and thought that Ira did a wonderful job writing it."

Ira Behr considers the episode a "character piece," not a comedy. "I know that sounds weird, but it was Quark suddenly being more than he was. He had a chance to be someone and what happens. I remember a friend of mine growing up who thought he was going to become a kid actor, someone had cast him as a part in a commercial and within a week he became the biggest son of a bitch on the earth. He was basically saying, 'I'm going to be a star, fuck all of you' and he meant it. His little head was turned

and I just thought it was interesting for Quark."

ALTMAN (***): "The Nagus" shows more promise than most of the recent DS9 voyages with some strong helming from David Livingston marking his first DS9 outing, witty writing from Ira Behr, and a fun performance from the always lively Wallace Shawn, who is brilliantly cast as the aged Ferengi royal. The B story involving Nog and Sisko's son, Jake, is enjoyable corn, although probably a little too mundane. It's another fine vehicle for Quark to the detriment of the rest of the ensemble.

GROSS (***): Inconceivable! An episode about the Ferengi that's actually enjoyable. Considering how absolutely annoying that race was when first introduced on TNG, it's nice to see how they've evolved from comic relief to fleshed-out beings. Wallace Shawn, perhaps best known for his role as The Sicilian in THE PRINCESS BRIDE, steals the show as the Nagus, a sleazy little toad of a Ferengi who is the epitome of the dirty old man with a wicked sense of humor. Armin Shimerman carries things nicely as Quark is temporarily elevated in status, though one wouldn't want to see a zany spin-off featuring the character. The B-story of

Jake secretly trying to teach Nog how to read, works surprisingly well.

Episode #11
"Vortex"

Original Airdate: 4/19/93
Written by Sam Rolfe
Directed by Winrich Kolbe

Guest Starring:
Cliff De Young (Corden), Randy Oglesby (Ah'Kel/Ro'Kel), Max Grodenchik (Rom), Kathleen Garrett (Vulcan Captain), Leslie Engelberg (Yareth), Gordon Clapp (Hadran)

After accidentally killing one of two Miradorn twins, an alien named Croden is placed under arrest by Odo. The surviving twin, Ah-Kel, vows vengeance and, in fact, his home world, Rakhar, demands that Croden be brought back to stand trial. Croden, the government emphasizes, is a criminal.

Throughout his capture, Croden tries to convince Odo that there is a colony of shape shifters that he knows of, and he reveals a small crystal medallion that comes from the colony. Odo isn't convinced, despite his temptation to believe the story on face value, and absolutely refuses to release Croden in exchange for the colony's location.

Odo is given the assignment of taking Croden back to

Rakhar, but enroute they are attacked by Ah-Kel's vessel. Croden leads them into a vortex to elude their pursuer, and gives Odo coordinates for the planet which is supposedly inhabited by the changelings. Once there, however, Odo discovers only Croden's daughter, who is in cyber-sleep. As Croden explains it, he is a criminal at home because he spoke out against the government. As a result, they slaughtered most of his family. Only he and his daughter barely got away.

The three take off in the Runabout, and Ah-Kel is tricked into using his weapons in an explosive area of the vortex, thus destroying himself. At the conclusion, Odo allows Croden and his daughter to beam over to a nearby Vulcan ship and safety. In return, he is given the crystal.

□□□□□

"A very effective episode," said Michael Piller. "Sam Rolfe is a legendary writer and I said, 'Sam, I want to do a western in which Odo has to go through the wormhole taking back a prisoner and has a relationship with the prisoner that explores his backstory and the tensions of what its like to be who he is.' He came up with a great story. I was mostly concerned that the sentimentality of the little girl on the planet was not going to play and that it was a

little hokum. Frankly, I think it really did play and I found it quite touching. I was intrigued with the mystery and the special effects they did in the vortex were sensational. It was one of the best in my book."

Said Ira Behr of the episode, "Where I was coming from was called SLEEPING DOGS, a New Zealand movie with Sam Neill and Warren Oates that Roger Donaldson directed. It's about a man who's living a mundane kind of life and there's political turmoil and the next thing he knows he's a wanted terrorist — and he hasn't done anything. It's a wonderful little movie and that's what we saw this guy as. Instead of being a criminal, he's a guy who woke up one day, and doesn't know why, but he did something wrong on his planet and they're after him now and he has to kill some people to get away from there. I thought it was a good Odo show. I think we could say it was one of the shows where, for whatever reason, we needed pyrotechnics at this point in the season. The whole thing with the vortex put me to sleep; it became tech."

Of more concern to actor Armin Shimerman was Quark's involvement with a murder in "Vortex" for which there were no consequences. Recalled Shimerman, "I had this chat with Rick Berman

and I asked him if we went over the line by having Quark participating in a really high crime. I thought that that was, and then not having to pay for his actions at the end....I thought that might be a little dangerous for the character and for the show because it means that he can get away with murder, which is not what I think the show is about, and it also makes somewhat of a fool of Odo because for that to happen under his nose and to let it get by, and Sisko for that matter, lessens their characters, as well."

Added David Livingston, "I just thought the way Kolbe shot the cave sequence where they go find the daughter was done very cleverly. That's a very small set. Kolbe made it look huge and cavernous and as though there were a lot of different places and tunnels. He really filled it out. It was just a very imaginative use of staging and camera."

ALTMAN (***): Although it's sappy and the residents of the Gamma Quadrant seem all too human, there's something strangely compelling about this story of a Rakhari criminal, Croden (Cliff De Young), who attempts to convince Odo that he knows where other shape-shifters like himself exist, deceiving the constable in order to reunite with his young daughter.

I'm not sure if it's just the 90's or Michael Piller's emphasis on "family values," but this STAR TREK, like its progenitors, is clearly a product of its times. Where else could you see an alien murderer turn out to be a simple family man at heart? What struck me the most about "Vortex" is the impressive scope of the production. There is a feature-film quality to it with some remarkable visual effects and sets, as well as the brief appearance of the Vulcans, which give the universe of STAR TREK in this show a refreshing breadth and diversity. I still believe if anything will date the show, it's the use of the tired morphing "shape shifting" gag which was old before it was new, but here exploiting the loneliness of Odo's existence as a changeling is well-played, giving the character a depth that it hadn't had until now. Much of the credit goes to Rene Auberjonois who has excelled in every moment of screen time he's had on the series. While the character may not be as appealing as Data, Auberjonois is certainly the Brent Spiner of this series...and yes, that's definitely a compliment.

GROSS (**1/2): Probably most interesting about this episode

is seeing the seemingly incorruptible Odo being tempted by the possibility of meeting others of his kind and learning something of his origin. This aspect of the show — and Rene Auberjonois' quiet display of the character's desperation to know the truth — is rather touching. The rest of the story is pretty standard STAR TREK fare (albeit with great effects), although Odo allowing his prisoner to escape to a Vulcan vessel is probably as significant a character moment as Data firing a phaser out of seeming vengeance in TNG's "The Most Toys."

Episode #12
"Battle Lines"

Original Airdate: 4/26/93
Story by Hilary Bader
Teleplay by Richard Danus and Evan Carlos Somers
Directed by Paul Lynch

Guest Starring:
Jonathan Banks (Shel-La),
Camille Saviola (Kai Opaka),
Paul Collins (Zlangco)

Sisko, Kira and Bashir take Kai Opaka on a trip through the wormhole, and are forced to crashland on an alien world, resulting in the death of the Kai. As they attempt to communicate with DS9, the survivors encounter two warring factions who are engaged in an endless conflict as an

alteration to their body chemistry and rendered them immortal — they can never die. This point is brought home when Kai Opaka revives, and finds herself trapped on this planet as well.

Although Bashir theorizes a possible cure for these people and Sisko is willing to bend the Prime Directive to allow him to use it, they are never given the opportunity when a rescue Runabout arrives and those at war make it clear that they're not ready to give up their battle just yet.

□□□□□

"'Battle Lines' is a good show," said Ira Behr. "We say goodbye to the Kai and we have some action. While it's not THE WILD BUNCH, it'll do. We have some vicious little fighting going on, hand to hand. People getting their throats cut and wounded and bleeding. It's an interesting show and I like it."

"I think this is one of the best premises of the season," said Michael Piller, who has apparently never seen "Day of the Dove." "For all those people who have written in and said we want more alien violence and sex, this is the episode. [Former intern] Hilary Bader is another one of those people who just keeps coming up with one good fresh idea after another. Now I have to do 56 of them next year. This was a great idea about a planet where you can never die ... it's a great premise for a science-fiction show and we put Kai Opaka on there and she becomes a fundamental part of this tale. It's about rebirth and resurrection and spiritual mystical things. One of the things I felt about this season is that I'm finding people react very positively to the mystical component of the pilot of DEEP SPACE NINE. I didn't do a lot more of them on DS9 after we set it up on the pilot, but this is one of them. My feeling is we should be finding more of those kinds of things. I think they're more interesting than ships breaking down."

Said Rick Berman, "Jonathan Banks did a nice job and there's some wonderful action in it. We deal with the death of the Kai and the rebirth of the Kai. I thought the concept of a punishment that is based on a microbe that allows these warring factions to never die was fascinating, and the idea that you have to constantly be recreating these battles and fighting one another. There was a lot of technobabble in it that got very complex, but I thought by and large that it was quite nice."

"Battle Lines" was the rewrite that got Evan Somers hired on staff for the season. "I started working on 'Battle Lines' before the pilot aired

and I saw the pilot and it confirmed some notions I had. I did a little rewriting and it was an elucidating experience. We were forming a new show and I was asked to come in and rewrite an episode that was an incredibly strong story that was dealing with characters I was fairly unfamiliar with. It was an interesting experience."

One of the writers on the show suggested that this episode was an attempt to sideline Opaka, who the staff had big plans for, but after being disappointed by Camille Saviola's performance in the pilot, it was time to send her off into the final frontier.

Said David Livingston, "I worked with Jonathan Banks on OTHERWORLD at Universal. That's where I knew him originally. Then I knew his work with BEVERLY HILLS COP, and then of course on WISEGUY. He is very odd and unusual actor, and he wears this wonderful makeup and did a terrific job. There are wonderful fight sequences with a lot of action. It's a very strong episode visually. The crew was exhausted after that episode having to work on Stage 18 in the dirt and in those caves and cramped quarters. It's very trying."

ALTMAN (★★ 1/2): "Battle Lines" begins with an enjoyable teaser in which the Kai

pays an unexpected visit to the station while Kira comes to terms with being a "minor terrorist", this according to the Cardassians. The more rousing elements of the show's first thirty minutes are offset by a less than satisfying resolution. Most notable is how inconsequential the Kai's role in the episode plays. After a fair amount of hand-wringing, it becomes apparent that Opaka being stranded on the planet is utterly pointless, serving very little dramatic purpose in the episode, except to allow for future episodes which address the power vacuum created by her exile.

Kira's moments with the Kai prove overly melodramatic, although Bashir finally gets to show his teeth. Tech credits are all commendable including Paul Lynch's best directing turn yet on the show, his p.o.v. shot from the turbo-lift as it descends is a particularly nice touch as is some well-done fight choreography. Strong performances by WISEGUY's Jonathan Banks as Shel-la and Avery Brooks' best outing yet as Sisko are also notable. I've already had enough of the spiritual Bajoran's prophecy...and being right about it. DS9 is validating their beliefs which is a trap it should avoid at all costs.

GROSS (★★★): Nice to see — at

last — a tie-in to the pilot in terms of the Kai's appearance. It's also about time that the wormhole is used to take us to a new planet and adventure — too bad that world happens to exist in a STAR TREK re-run. Yet despite story similarities to TREK classic's "Day of the Dove," "Battle Lines" works rather well, helped considerably by the fact that the warring factions are motivated by a determination to vanquish their opponents — despite the futility of their efforts — rather than being influenced by an alien presence. Even when Bashir can potentially offer them freedom by death, their first impulse is to use the doctor's theory as a weapon against the enemy. The coda, in which Sisko basically leaves them to fend for themselves, is a rather downbeat conclusion for a STAR TREK episode.

There are a couple of nice character moments, particularly between Kira and the Kai, with Kira coming to grips with the position she currently occupies. Also, there's a wonderful scene between Sisko and Bashir regarding the Prime Directive that sounds like it could have taken place between Kirk and McCoy.

**Episode #13
"The Storyteller"**

Original Airdate: 5/3/93

**Story by
Kurt Michael Bensmiller
Teleplay by
Kurt Michael Bensmiller and
Ira Steven Behr
Directed by David Livingston**

**Guest Starring:
Kay E. Kuter (The Sirah),
Lawrence Monoson (Hovath),
Jim Jansen (Faren), Gina
Philips (Varis), Aron Eisenberg
(Nog), Jordan Lund (Woban),
Amy Benedict (Woman)**

While responding to a medical emergency in a small Bajoran village, O'Brien, who has accompanied Dr. Bashir, is pronounced by the dying Sirah to have been sent by the Prophets. It has been the Sirah's task to tell a tale to the village as the cloud-like Dal'Rok unleashed its fury, but as he collapses during an attack, he tells O'Brien how to fight off the manifestation and O'Brien is successful. When the Sirah dies, the villagers announce that O'Brien will be taking his place, and they start to worship him like a god.

This places O'Brien's life in danger, as he barely avoids an attack by Hovath, the former Sirah's apprentice, who claims that he should have been the man's successor. Naturally, O'Brien is happy to give up the "throne" and he works with Hovath to make this happen, as the young man sends the

Dal'Rok away and captures the respect of his people.

ooooo

"It was very difficult to shoot and we were way over budget on the opticals on that show because of the complexity of this thing that appears in the sky," said Rick Berman. "It was a little fanciful but I think the science-fiction element involving a creature created by the collective imagination of this village as a way of bringing them closer together, and it having to do with a little piece of one of the orbs that is held by the Storyteller, was a very interesting concept."

Frances Praksti [STAR RUNNERS] played one of the Bajoran women that was presented to O'Brien as a "gift" from the village. In an audition with 75 other girls she had to convincingly "give" herself to director David Livingston. "It took about an hour to do my nose and once I had it on, it felt really comfortable. David Livingston was great, he didn't stop until he got exactly what he wanted. He didn't settle for good, it had to be perfect and we must have done it about 21 times. I liked Colm and Siddig, who I felt bad for because he ate 15 kiwis in that scene until we got it right. He said he'd never eat one again."

Laughed El Fadil of his close encounter with the kiwi

of the worst kind, "That stuff burnt my mouth. I've satiated myself on fruit before and I never had that sensation before. I don't know how many I had. They counted, it was somewhere in the region of the twenties within an hour. I had to put stuff on my lips because the citric acid went right through. I don't ever want to do that again. Next time, I'll be happy to do something mild like a glass of milk."

ALTMAN (***): Although the "evil entity" menace plays like a bad science-fiction 50's B-movie contrivance, the juice of the episode is the Abbott & Costello banter between Chief O'Brien and Dr. Bashir. Both Meaney and El Fadil are delightful, with Bashir taking devilish delight in O'Brien's MAN WHO WOULD BE KING-predicament. The B-story involving Jake and Nog's affinity for a comely young Bajoran is surprisingly entertaining, distinguished by a moment of comic inspiration in which Nog hurls a bucket of oatmeal at the young Sisko who thinks it's Odo in his disassembled form. David Livingston once again proves he's one of the show's foremost helmers in this logistically daunting installment, bringing both grandeur to the effects-laden scenes on Bajor as well as a new vitality to the

Director David Livingston with a model version of the set for "The Storyteller"

station-bound moments aboard Deep Space Nine.

GROSS (**1/2): Maybe it's me, but I feel like "The Storyteller" is, largely, a remake of "The Nagus," substituting O'Brien for Quark. Despite this, there's some fun to be gotten here, particularly between Bashir and O'Brien and the situation aboard the space station between the kids. There's also some humor to be gotten from O'Brien being deemed something of a savior to these people, but this is not an outstanding episode from any point of view, with the exception of the opportunities it offers Colm Meaney and Siddig El Fadil in their scenes together. Oh, yeah. There are some neat Spielbergian cloud effects too.

Episode #14
"Progress"

Original Airdate: 5/9/93
Written by Peter Allan Fields
Directed by Les Landau

Guest Starring:
Brian Keith (Mullibok), Aron Eisenberg (Nog), Nicholas Worth (Alien Captain), Michael Bofshever (Toran), Daniel Riordan (1st Guard), Terrence Evans (Baltrim), Annie O'Donnell (Keena)

A Bajorn farmer, Mullibok (Brian Keith), refuses to vacate his farm on a Bajoran moon which has been evacuated so that the Bajor can harness its natural energy for the benefit of its citizenry.

When a Bajoran farm on the moon of Jeraddo has to be evacuated so that a large-scale energy transfer tapping that moon's core can be executed, Kira and Dax travel there to make sure that everyone is gone. What they find is a stubborn farmer named Mullibok, along with Baltrim and Keena, who refuses to leave, even if his life is in danger. After some time passes, Dax returns to DS9 while Kira remains behind to try and convince the man of the threat.

As time goes on, Kira and Mullibok bond with each other, with Kira even coming to the point where she considers abandoning her responsibilities so that the man can live out the rest of his life here. In the end, though — particularly after Sisko has beamed down told her that she's no longer the underdog, that she represents something more to the people of Bajor — she realizes she must carry out her duty, even if that means burning down Mullibok's home and taking the man against his will.

□□□□□

"In the middle part of the year, we suddenly realized we had sort of lost Kira, which is immediately taken care of with this and several other episodes as the season goes on," said Michael Piller. "Brian Keith was the guest star and I think it's very nice casting. I think it brings a certain reputation to your series when actors of quality choose to guest star

on it. It's a very personal story and it's a story that's been oft told in contemporary times, and I think people relate to it. Our attempt was to show a softer side of Kira that would expand her character and I think we do in a marvelous way. It's really a two man show, in a sense, but there's also a great scene between Kira and Sisko."

Added Rick Berman, "I think it turned out real nice. The end is rather bittersweet. Brian Keith gave a performance that was very interesting and was in many ways better than I expected. It's a very poignant story in the relationship between Major Kira and this old man."

"I think it's a great show for Kira," offered Ira Steven Behr. "We've done fairly well with everyone this season. And we even gave Jake and Nog three B-stories. I always wanted to do Milo Minderbinder from CATCH-22, the guy who can acquire things and we put these two kids together as the Milo Minderbinders of DEEP SPACE NINE and it has some nice stuff in it."

Commented David Livingston, "It's an eminent domain story and it's charming. Brian Keith was terrific. We couldn't give Les and Marvin all the set we wanted to give them, so they had to

come up with ways of shooting this set to make the exterior look believable. I think they did a great job."

ALTMAN (***): Peter Fields' passionate script is superbly written and it's easy to empathize with Kira's dilemma. Brian Keith gives a moving performance as farmer Mullibok and his sarcastic retorts are stinging. The Jake and Nog B-story involving their first business venture is surprisingly engaging. Unfortunately, the episode's ambiguous conclusion is less satisfying and Kira's torching of the farmer's abode brings up several troubling moral questions which the episode fails to address. The character drama is finally coming together on the show as evidenced by a powerful scene between Sisko and Kira on the planet — although those who enjoy STAR TREK for its science-fiction rather than philosophical content are bound to be sorely disappointed thus far in the season.

GROSS (***1/2): Uncle Bill is back, but where is Mr. French? (You've got to be a real couch potato to understand that one.) In the process of trying to complete a mission, Kira touches a part of herself that has been missing for most of her life. In coming into the existence lived by Mullibok, Kira is at first resistant to but gradually embraces an idyllic lifestyle so unlike her experience as, first, a resistance fighter and then the first officer of DS9. Here is a simpler life, one untouched by the realities of war.

The interaction between Brian Keith and Nana Visitor — particularly Keith's early jabs at Visitor — is wonderful, and the major's internal conflict a realistic one. Her ultimate decision to force Mullibok to leave the planet by torching his home is an honest one, going directly against the typical Hollywood (and oftentimes STAR TREK) coda which would have had her find a way for him to remain behind.

Episode #15
"If Wishes Were Horses"

Original Airdate: 5/17/93
Story by
Neil McCue Crawford
and William Crawford
Teleplay by
Neil McCue Crawford
& William Crawford
and Michael Piller
Directed by Rob Legato

Guest Starring:
Keone Young (Buck Bokai), Rosalind Chao (Keiko), Hana Hatae (Molly), Michael John Anderson (Rumpelstiltskin)

The imagination of DS9 crewmembers start to manifest themselves in real life.

O'Brien, who has read the tale of "Rumpelstiltskin" to his daughter, is suddenly confronted by the dwarf; Sisko meets up with baseball legend Buck Bokai, who for the first time has stepped out of the holodeck program created by the commander and is carrying on conversations with him as though they're the dearest of friends; and Bashir imagines a new version of Dax who is completely submissive and wants nothing more than to please him. At the same time, the space station is threatened by a rip in space that seems to be sucking everything into it.

All of it turns out to be the work of alien beings who have tapped in to the human imagination in order to gain a fuller understanding of the species.

□□□□□

"It was a very hard concept to make work," said Michael Piller. "Somebody came in and said Jake brings a baseball player home from the holodeck, and that was the pitch. Basically, I said we just did the Moriarty show where he walks out of the holodeck in NEXT GENERATION and I didn't want to do another holodeck show, but I would like to do a show that celebrates imagination since that's really what STAR TREK is, a celebration of the imagination. We knew it was sort of a [TNG

first season's] 'Where No One Has Gone Before' concept, but that was six years ago on another show, so why can't we do something where strange things are happening that people are imagining?"

One figment of Michael Piller's imagination that never made it to the screen was his decision to have O'Brien's story to his daughter be that of a leprechaun, the fictional Irish dwarf with a pot of gold. Said Piller, "We needed a reason for it to be happening and we came up with the idea that O'Brien would be telling a bedtime story about a Leprechaun. We had the script written and Colm Meaney called Rick and said, 'Every Irish actor I know has worked his entire life trying to overcome the stereotype of Irish people and leprechauns. It's really racist and I don't want to do it.' We had no idea there was any sensitivity to leprechaun in the Irish culture and certainly we did not want to force Colm Meaney to act with a leprechaun, but what the hell do you do after you've got a whole story structured around a leprechaun stealing a child? Well, we went through story tales and Robert [Wolfe] came in with Rumpelstiltskin (Michael John Anderson) and we went by it at least once, maybe twice, because Rumpelstiltskin wasn't exactly the same thing and wouldn't work in the structure we had. When I finally sat down to rewrite it, I said okay Rumpelstiltskin — let's see where it goes. It was one of those scripts where I had no idea how to resolve it [or] where it was going to go. I wrote each scene to see if it worked and had fun with it."

Piller noted of the scenes of the romantic rendezvous between Bashir and his dream Dax, "I've saved the dailies of where Terry's coming onto Siddig and he doesn't know why for my personal collection. There were 12 takes and he kept breaking up and fluffing his lines."

Commented Armin Shimerman who had the challenge of acting with two voluptuous fantasy girls, "The writers were kind enough to give me every adolescent's fantasy. They gave me these two beautiful women who were very sweet. It was fun."

"This is an episode which you've got to try and do," said Ira Behr. "We should be awarded brass balls for doing Rumpelstiltskin. It's an interesting show and it has a level of imagination and it's a high concept. Sometimes they work and sometimes they don't."

ALTMAN (1/2):** An overbaked stew of every TREK cliché imaginable in which the

Avery Brooks takes command of DS9 as Benjamin Sisko (photo copyright ©1994 Gamma Liaison)

crew's imaginations give life to their innermost fantasies, resulting in an all-too-real threat to the station — only to find out that the enigmatic visions are aliens visiting the station to learn more about human's and their pesky dreams.

Riddled with technobabble, "If Wishes Were Horses" makes the wise decision to derive its illusions from its characters, which is what provides the episode's emotional juice. Bashir's fantasies involving Dax are a comedic triumph and Terry Farrell is particularly adept at the lighter moments. The scenes between Sisko and baseball player Buck Bokai (Keone Young) have a surprising degree of emotional resonance, although I am dubious of Piller's postulation that baseball's future is in jeopardy. What could have been a charming and emotionally revealing episode suffers from the misstep of saddling the show with a menacing jeopardy plot. You'd think after NEXT GENERATION's fifth season, they'd know better.

GROSS (**): In tonight's episode of STAR TREK: VOY-AGER, the crew of the USS Voyager are hard-pressed to explain illusions which seem to spring from their minds.....sorry, just took a trip back to the future and read a couple of issues of TV GUIDE, which detailed this intriguing plot of the next TREK series, which, incidentally, followed the one in which nearly the entire crew was stricken with a disease that nearly destroyed the ship, until the doctor found a solution in the last few critical seconds.

Earnest performances save "If Wishes Were Horses" from being a complete disaster, but the whole premise of the episode reeks of TREKs past. There are moments to be had here, particularly those within the Dax/Bashir/Dax "triangle," but not much more. Better luck next time (and one would imagine that there will definitely be a next time).

Episode #16
"The Forsaken"

Story by Jim Trombetta
Teleplay by Carlos Dunaway and Michael Piller
Directed by Les Landau

Guest Starring:
Majel Barrett (Lwaxana Troi), Constance Towers (Ambassador Taxco), Michael Ensign (Ambassador Lojai), Jack

Shearer (Ambassador Vadosia), Benita Andre (Anara)

When the Deep Space Nine computer is infected by an alien presence, all of O'Brien's attempts to get rid of it are fruitless. As a result, various items cease working properly, including the transporter and turbolifts, which in turn has an effect on Odo that he doesn't take kindly to: trapping him aboard a turbolift with Lwaxana Troi, one of the ambassadors who are on the station.

As O'Brien tries to figure a way out of this situation, Bashir handles three diplomats while Odo and Troi open up to each other in surprising ways, culminating in Odo's having to return to his original form and her promising to take care of him.

☐☐☐☐☐

"It started out being called 'Ghost In the Machine,'" said Evan Somers. "I was here back in the fall when the trio of ideas was pitched and sold — and it was quite a remarkable day — by a writer named Jim Trombetta. This is the first that had come to the point where a treatment had been submitted that was adequate to break. The story that had been initially pitched was relegated to B story category, and a very interesting A story emerged involving Lwaxana Troi and Odo.

Michael just did some brilliant work writing that."

"That was the only element of that story that really appealed to me when we first heard it," said Michael Piller of Mrs. Troi's freshman visit to DS9. "We were looking for A/B/C stories that gave us the opportunity to do lots of little stories in that same 'life on the space station' vein. We were also looking for bottle shows to save money. This does fit into the category of the season where it was time to start paying the piper. I figured putting two people in an elevator has got to save money somewhere. The idea of having an enemy go into the computer is certainly not a new one, but I think we found a different spin on it and we've got some very interesting comedy from Siddig and his tour of ambassadors. The ensemble seemed to be working much better for me by this time and I just think that stuff in the elevator will be talked about forever. It's a wonderful performance by Rene, and Majel was at her warmest and most wonderful as Mrs. Troi. She goes from being the woman you can't imagine being stuck in an elevator with to the best companion you could possibly ever have."

Said Rick Berman, "I think here's another example of bringing a character from NEXT GENERATION that is delightful.

Rene remains one of my favorite actors of all time and he does a wonderful job here. It's remarkably poignant."

"It was great working with Majel Barrett," said Armin Shimerman. "I looked forward to doing that. She was sweet, she was kind and she was funny. She was so at home on these sets. It really looked like someone coming home to roost. The crew adores her and she was so considerate. Considering her position in the cosmology of STAR TREK, she was a very, very considerate person."

And what does Marina Sirtis think of her fictional mother's latest TREK? "I'm pissed," said Sirtis of Mrs. Troi, who didn't visit the Enterprise sixth season. "She's my mother, she should be on *my* show."

Majel Barrett delivered one of her best performances as Mrs. Troi in "The Forsaken" (photo copyright ©1994 Karen Witkowski)

ALTMAN (***): Some of the best writing of the season by Michael Piller and lively performances by Rene Auberjonois and Majel Barrett make this story of a computer program which causes havoc on the station, and trapping Mrs. Troi and Odo in a turbolift, a worthwhile installment.

While the pathos involving a dissolving Odo and Mrs. Troi is effectively realized, Piller's script is laden with several other strong character-driven exchanges between Troi and her would-be paramour as well as a pleasantly offbeat C story involving Bashir's tour of the station for a coterie of insufferable visiting Federation ambassadors. Less palatable is the computer virus macguffin, although Colm Meaney's earnest acting almost makes the storyline seem credible. One gnawing flaw, however, is the fact that both TNG and DS9 have yet to get the Vulcans right no matter how hard they've tried. Jack Shearer as Vulcan ambassador Vadosia is just dreadful.

GROSS (***1/2): Let's handle the storylines backwards. The "C"-story, humorous. The computer-virus "B"-story, a rather cliched macguffin, but what a wonderful "A"-story it leads in to. Never having been much of a fan of Mrs. Troi (though that was dispelled in her last few visits to the Enterprise during seasons five and six), it's delightful to see her in such fine form. Trapping Troi and Odo in the turbolift seems like the most contrived method of creating a bottle show imaginable, yet the writing of Carlos

Dunaway and Michael Piller, as well as Les Landau's intimate direction, brings these characters to life in new and unexpected ways as each gradually strips away the facades that they normally wear so proudly, and reveal their inner selves.

A real highlight is Rene Auberjonois' quiet desperation in trying to resist the transformation into his base self, and Majel Barrett's gentle assurance that she will take care of him.

Episode #17
"Dramatis Personae"

Original Airdate: 5/31/93
Written by Joe Menosky
Directed by Cliff Bole

Guest Starring:
Tom Towles (Klingon), Stephen Parr (Valerian), Randy Pflug (Guard), Jeff Pruitt (Ensign)

The telepathic energy of a destroyed species in the Gamma Quadrant takes over the crew of DS9 forcing them to re-enact the Shakesperean power struggle which destroyed their world. What it basically comes down to is the Federation against the Bajorans, in particular Sisko's heading one faction and Kira the other. Odo, being the only person not affected by the alien influence, manages to manipulate Bashir into using a cure that rids of the crew of the extraterrestrial presence, which is then blown out of an airlock.

ΟΟΟΟΟ

"It was a lot of fun," said actress Nana Visitor, who plots against Commander Sisko's life as she assumes a sexier, more vicious persona. "It was interesting to see how used to each other and the characters we've been playing we are. To see Avery behaving in a certain way and Siddig and Terry in a very different mindset was fun. I came and watched scenes I wasn't involved with just to see what was going on."

"We got Menosky back to do a script," said Michael Piller of the former TNG Executive Script Consultant who left DS9's sister series to take a sabbatical in Europe last year. "It's somewhat of a low budget affair, but a very interesting one with great performances. It's a very perverted little episode and I think entertaining. Cliff, who very much wanted to direct DS9 for us, came in and finally got to direct this one and did a wonderful job."

Said Visitor of first-time DS9 director Cliff Bole, a TNG veteran, "Cliff was wonderful because he's got a great sense of humor. He doesn't take himself too seriously and yet he commands respect so you feel you're safe and are going to be taken care of and watched out for so that you can take some chances. Then you can do something that might be great and might be awful, but he'll be there to tell you that didn't work or it's great. That's the only way you can do interesting stuff. If you're always playing it safe, it gets boring, for me anyway, and I think for most actors. He was great and he had a very low-key attitude which I really enjoyed."

Piller didn't feel that having the characters take on new personas while they were still developing first season was a mistake. "It's dangerous, but the reason we were able to do that was because we had developed them so well the first half of the season," he said. "If you go back to the first season of NEXT GENERATION, people were changing and you had viruses changing them into horny people — so I suppose its not that unusual."

"I love this episode," enthused Armin Shimerman. "I love the fact that revolution broke. Even though it wasn't a real revolution, I still love the conflict between Sisko and Major Kira, a person who is a national and who only thinks of her world first. I love those issues of nationalism because we go through that here in Los Angeles a lot. We had our riots because neighborhoods felt that they weren't getting a fair share of the wealth of Los

Angeles and there's the Bajorans who are fighting because they're not getting a fair share of what they think they deserve. That's very intrinsic to the life we live in Los Angeles so when it's represented on television, I feel for that."

ALTMAN (**): While the idea of an alien mind probe taking over isn't a new concept, the idea of its manifestation creating a *literal* "power play" aboard the station makes it a captivating conceit. Regrettably, the "Mirror, Mirror"-like dynamics of the feuding factions play out far too tamely and are hurt by a number of surprisingly weak performances lacking the spit and vinegar of the political showdowns in that classic original TREK episode to which this bears a passing resemblance. Ultimately, the episode is devoid of passion, simply functioning as a tame bottle show when it had the potential to be far more compelling with some genuine conflict.

GROSS (*1/2): Listen closely. Hear that munching sound? That's the sound made by actors chewing the scenery, and there's a lot of that going on around in this episode, which wouldn't be so bad if the storyline giving them cause

to munch wasn't such old-hat. Some fun moments, but all in all, not a real season highlight.

Episode #18
"Duet"

Original Airdate: 6/14/93
Story by Lisa Rich
& Jeanne Carrigan Fauci
Teleplay by Peter Allan Fields
Directed by James L. Conway

Guest Starring:
Marc Alaimo (Gul Dukat), Ted Sorel (Kaval), Tony Rizzoli (Kainon), Norman Large (Captain), Robin Christopher (Neela), Harris Yulla (Marritza)

Kira is stunned when a Cardassian war criminal appears at the station, bragging of the atrocities he committed against the Bajoran people. Kira, naturally, wants him sent to Bajor to stand trial and be executed, but Sisko isn't so sure that the man is who he claims to be.

All of the station's resources are pulled together to investigate the man's tale and certain inaccuracies in his statements. What they eventually discover is that he is actually Marritza, a simple filing clerk who, in his own words, did not have the courage to come up from under a table where he wept upon hearing the screams of Bajorans being slaughtered. Ironically, Kira starts to feel sorry for him and

starts to discuss possibilities for the future, when a Bajoran leaps out of hiding and stabs him to death, not caring who he was — only driven by the fact that the man was a Cardassian. As such, he deserved to die.

□□□□□

"I'd like to say that my performance as Marritza in Pete's office was absolutely brilliant," joked Ira Behr of his animated breaking of the script with co-producer Peter Fields. "I only wish the cameras were rolling. I'm very, very proud of this show. Not in the sense that it's a show for all humanity, but that it was a fun show to work on. You had a character who was larger than life and is reveling in his evilness. It was just a blast. It was a lot of fun to write, but it was the end of the season and we were all very tired, so neither Peter or I were very happy doing it. We work very well together and the show could have, literally, been another half hour if they would have let us. It was just mind games on mind games and we could have done that forever."

Commented Michael Piller of the bottle show, "We had to come up with some very creative ways to do shows that did not cost a lot of money. This was pitched to us by two of our interns who wanted to do something about a war criminal. In the context it was pitched, it didn't turn me on. The idea of a war criminal found aboard DS9 seemed to me to be an interesting concept, but at first it seemed to me to be a JUDGMENT AT NUREMBERG court show. We had done 'Dax' and didn't want to do another courtroom show. Ira gave us the twist that gave it THE MAN IN THE GLASS BOOTH kind of feeling, where the guy isn't who is he says he is, but is doing it for more noble reasons. The writing is really quite powerful and it's going to send some shivers down some spines. The last two episodes of the season are very thought provoking."

"I've always been a big fan of Harris Yulin's," said Armin Shimerman. "We were acquaintances years ago when I first met my wife. We were all doing Broadway together. It's a fascinating episode dealing with Bajor and nationalism and with Cardassian war crimes. I love these kind of scripts because they deal with social issues using the context of space to deal with them."

Nana Visitor shares the enthusiasm of the rest of the ensemble for STAR TREK's tradition of addressing important contemporary issues in the guise of science-fiction. "The action comes out of big issues on this show," she said. "There's action and intrigue, but the writing really lets us

The Cardassians pay a visit to their old stomping ground, Deep Space Nine (photo copyright ©1994 David Strick/Onyx)

deal with issues we're not embarrassed to commit ourselves to as actors and people. On a sitcom, very often it's should I let Johnny stay out after midnight or not? It's an important issue, but not quite so much as Holocaust victims and facing evil in one persona and how you deal with that, which is one thing that I had to deal with in 'Duet.' It was kind of harrowing to have to deal with that subject matter every day, but the harder it is, the more rewarding it is."

ALTMAN (*1/2):** Like TNG's "The Drumhead," "Duet" proves that a little money can go a long way in this story of a Cardassian who comes to DS9 and is believed by Kira to be war criminal Gul Darheel, the commandant of a Cardassian prison labor camp.

As good as Nana Visitor is in the penultimate episode of the season, Harris Yulin is nothing short of a revelation as Marritza, the Cardassian prisoner who may or may not be the perpetrator of heinous crimes against the Bajoran people. While the episode's Holocaust allegory is a little too on the nose, the crisp writing by Peter Allan Fields along with vibrant direction from Jim Conway and a moving coda make the story one of the year's highlights, showcasing the characters — and the show — at its best.

GROSS (****): There are bottle shows and then there are bottle shows, and "Duet" probably represents the best that the form has to offer. Peter Allan Fields has written what is probably his finest script, and director James

Conway has done his share in bringing the episode to riveting life. Naturally, though, it is the performances of Nana Visitor and, particularly, Harris Yulin that hit home. Their scenes together are electric, capturing Kira's fury and Marritza's initial, arrogance and ultimately pitiable qualities.

Above all else, "Duet" proves that you don't need high concepts, heavy doses of science fiction plotlines or encyclopedias of technobabble to make a great episode. Two people in a room will do it, if only you give them the written material, direction and actors to make it happen. Easily DEEP SPACE NINE's greatest first season triumph.

Episode #19
"In the Hands of the Prophets"

Original Airdate: 6/21/93
Written by
Robert Hewitt Wolfe
Directed by David Livingston

Guest Starring:
Rosalind Chao (Keiko O'Brien), Philip Anglim (Vedek Barrell), Robin Christopher (Neela), Michael Eugene Fairman (Vendor), Louise Fletcher (Winn)

Shortly after the arrival of Bajoran spiritual leader, Vedek Winn, who is vying to become Kai, a division begins to occur between the Bajorans and other races residing on Deep Space Nine. When Winn's views are not readily accepted, sabotage in the form of explosions and even murder begins to occur, leading up to the attempted assassination of the visiting Vedek Bereil, who happens to be Winn's primary competition in becoming Kai. What ultimately unfolds is that Winn's rhetoric is more politically than spiritually motivated.

ㅁㅁㅁㅁㅁ

In picking her favorite episode of the season, Nana Visitor noted, "I'd probably always say the last episode we filmed was my absolute favorite because I'm always still caught up in that archetype that I am working in. One of the most fun things was the last scene of the last show between Avery and me when I am going, 'Wow, I can't believe that just a year ago I was in such a different place and now I'm wearing this uniform.' It was fun because it was the last scene of the season and it was with Avery and we looked at each other and kind of had a moment of realizing we really had gone through something here. The day that we filmed that was my son's first birthday and when I was going, 'Wow, I'd never believe I was wearing this uniform', I could totally let that be truthful, because a year ago, at that hour, I was giving birth."

Said Ira Behr, "We have four shows next season that we're planning which are outgrowths of 'In The Hands Of The Prophets.' On one level, you could just say we're doing INHERIT THE WIND, but I think it enables us as a specific television series, DS9, to explore the Bajoran spiritual life which we haven't done to much of. It's one of the things we talked about, which is the rational scientific bent of the Federation versus the Bajoran spiritual outlook on life which is a clash that I think can give us episodes for quite some time."

"The last episode is really the showdown between the humanist ideals of the Federation and the religious spiritual philosophy of Bajor," said Michael Piller, who did the uncredited rewrite on the teleplay. "It provides a bookend to the season that has a confrontation that seems to have been coming all along when we met these people and found out what their lives were like. You start to deal with religion in school, school prayer, the Scopes monkey trial and fundamentalism and it's very thought provoking — and may get a letter or two."

Added Piller with a smile, referring to the deluge of mail TNG received after Worf went hunting in BIRTHRIGHT, "All I should do is send out the high priestess and have her kill an animal and then I'll *really* get some letters."

Said staff writer Robert Wolfe, who will be returning second season, "I think for a first season we accomplished a lot and did a lot of good things. It took us a little while to get some of the bugs worked out but I think we're doing a great job now. Next year I would like to see different combinations of characters than we've seen so far this season; I'd like to see Sisko/Quark, Odo/Bashir, Kira/Dax, just to see how those characters clicked with each other. I think we're going to do some more of the political intrigue and some stuff will definitely come out of 'In The Hands of The Prophets' and that'll be great. It's tough, but now I just have to take a deep breath and start thinking about next season."

ALTMAN (***1/2): DEEP SPACE NINE finally defines itself and the show that has emerged is as philosophically compelling as any show on television today. Ironically, "Prophets" achieves a level of sophistication and social relevance which the original show prided itself on but never really displayed, except in the broadest of terms. No doubt "Prophets" will illustrate that DS9 may not be as palatable to some as previous TREKs, but has, in its last two episodes,

shown the viability of Berman and Piller's initial premise for the show, distinguishing it from its starship-bound brood. Avery Brooks finally breaks out of his laconic stupor and displays some passion in a speech that is as good as his "Man Alone" pontificating was bad. Louise Fletcher brings weight and legitimacy to the role of Vedek Winn, and David Livingston's slow motion assassination sequence, as well as the final shot of the season in ops, are both executed with finesse. As for Robin Christopher as Nella, is it a pre-requisite to be well-endowed to be stationed to DEEP SPACE NINE?

GROSS (***1/2): Although it took nearly the entire season (with a brief stopover during "Battle Lines"), DS9 finally connects back with the pilot episode in terms of dealing with Bajoran spirituality and the political struggles erupting on Bajor. There is an underly

ing tension surrounding the episode that begins from the moment that Louise Fletcher appears as Vedek Winn and continues right through the suspenseful attempted assassination of Vedek Barrell. Even during the closing scene between Sisko and Kira, where they discuss all that has been accomplished so far and their hope for the future, there is a sense that no one is too sure just how volatile the situation on Bajor will ultimately become. Thankfully all of this would successfully be carried over and explored further during DS9's three-part second season opener.

APPENDIX A

THE COMIC

One of the more exciting licensed products awaiting fans of the series is the monthly comic book from Malibu Comics. Written by TREK comic veteran, Mike W. Barr and illustrated by Gordon Percell, Malibu promises to re-energize TREK in the graphics medium.

"Mike Barr has a long association with STAR TREK and is the only writer to have written TREK at three different companies: Marvel, DC and now Malibu," said Tom Mason, Creative Director and editor of the DEEP SPACE NINE line at Malibu. "Mike is one of the biggest classic TREK fans that I've ever met. He knows TREK trivia backwards and forwards and knows a ton of goofy STAR TREK facts that people don't even think about. I'm not sure if he eats and breathes it, but he knows it and he knows how to take those elements and make them a convincing story. He doesn't focus on the minutia of STAR TREK, but takes it and adds it to a compelling story and makes it that much deeper."

Continued Mason, "When we got the license, we sat around and tried to figure out who we would get to do STAR TREK. One of the things we agreed on was we wanted to have a writer who had name value to STAR TREK fans, but also a guy who could tell a really good story in a complex context. This is not amateur night where we're going to round up the usual suspects and put out a cheesy STAR TREK comic. We invited Barr up here for lunch one afternoon without telling him why and he thought he was here about writing superhero comics. We got him on this tangent about STAR TREK and he went on and on and on about the show and how he was looking forward to DEEP SPACE NINE and his hopes for it. It was clear that he wanted to be involved...and should be involved. I just happened to mention that we were signing for the license and would he be interested in working on some ideas. Needless to say, he was."

Although Malibu can't make use of such characters as Captain Kirk and members of the original cast, there are certain elements from NEXT GENERATION that can be mined such as Q, Lwaxana Troi, Vash and even Jean Luc Picard since they have appeared on DEEP SPACE NINE. "If you like STAR TREK: DS9, there is no reason in the world you wouldn't like the DS9 comic book," said Mason. "It is essentially another episode of the TV show and you can expect good writing, good art and, more importantly, you can expect to learn things about the space station and the characters you haven't learned from the TV show."

Mason traced Malibu's interest in the TREK property to when the new show was first announced two years ago. "We all sat around saying we should get that because we had a lot of licensed properties in our stable but we were looking for a flagship license that would really boost up the image of the company," he said. "We thought it would be great if DS9 were available, but we thought since DC had CLASSIC TREK and STAR TREK: THE NEXT GENERATION, that it would be automatic that Paramount was going to give it to DC. But the more we thought it about it, the more we thought maybe it's not a given and that there was something we could do."

Malibu Publisher Scott Rosenberg was informed by Paramount that the studio's licensing division was willing to entertain bids from other companies which prompted the fifth-ranked comic company to prepare an extensive presentation featuring art, marketing proposals and a tour of their facilities. "First of all, a lot of us here are longtime STAR TREK fans and we knew the new series DS9 was coming out and we really wanted to do the comic," said Rosenberg. "We knew it would be difficult to get the license because DC has had it for eight years and Marvel for five years before that, and we knew it would be tough for a relatively new company like Malibu to get it. What we did is we commissioned some sample artwork and story pages and we met with about ten different people at Paramount, showing them what we could do with the comic that we thought would be different. We invited them to our offices to meet the whole team so they knew the actual people and faces that would be involved in putting together the comic. We talked over with them, in a roundtable format, all the different kinds of stories we could do and the marketing promotions and a lot of other things of that ilk. Finally, they made the decision

they were going to go with us for this one even though STAR TREK and NEXT GENERATION are still with DC."

Recalling the initial presentation, Mason commented, "Scott said the checkbook is open. We did some artwork, came up with a couple of story ideas, a promotional plan about how Malibu could support STAR TREK: DS9 with advertising and special covers and top-flight creators and superior production values, and all this stuff. We assembled it all and in less than a month we had full color art, a complete promotional campaign mapped out and sent Scott into Paramount in his best suit and tie and they talked dollars and cents. More important than that was that Paramount was interested in what we would do, as opposed to how much we would pay them, which I thought was impressive since I always think of companies as saying 'can you match this?'"

Comic readers are in for a treat with Malibu's sophisticated treatment of the DS9 property. In addition to the monthly comic, Mason hints as some special miniseries and spin-offs that are planned for the future [one of which,

"Hearts & Minds," will be written by Mark A. Altman]. Also being offered by the company are premium collectors' editions which will include limited edition gold and silver foil issues, a Circle K cup promotion for charity and a chance for fans to be drawn into the comic and win a trip to the Paramount lot.

"I essentially have an unlimited budget," said Mason. "I'm only limited to the writers' and artists' imagination. If I want to draw a giant spaceship, it costs just as much as two people standing around talking. I'm also not limited by sets so I want to explore the unknown parts of the space station and in the first issue we see what's on level fourteen, which was mentioned in the pilot as being where the Cardassians used to store things. I want to be able to open the station a little more and see where Quark is

when he's not working or where Odo is or what Dr. Bashir does for relaxation besides hunch over his microscope. I want to be able to see different facets of the characters which haven't been explored on the show."

Concluded Mason, "The way I wanted to view this comic book is that our stories are essentially unfilmed episodes of the TV show, that if DS9 is only doing 22 episodes a season, then Malibu is doing 12 more per year as a supplement so you get 34 episodes a year instead of the 22."

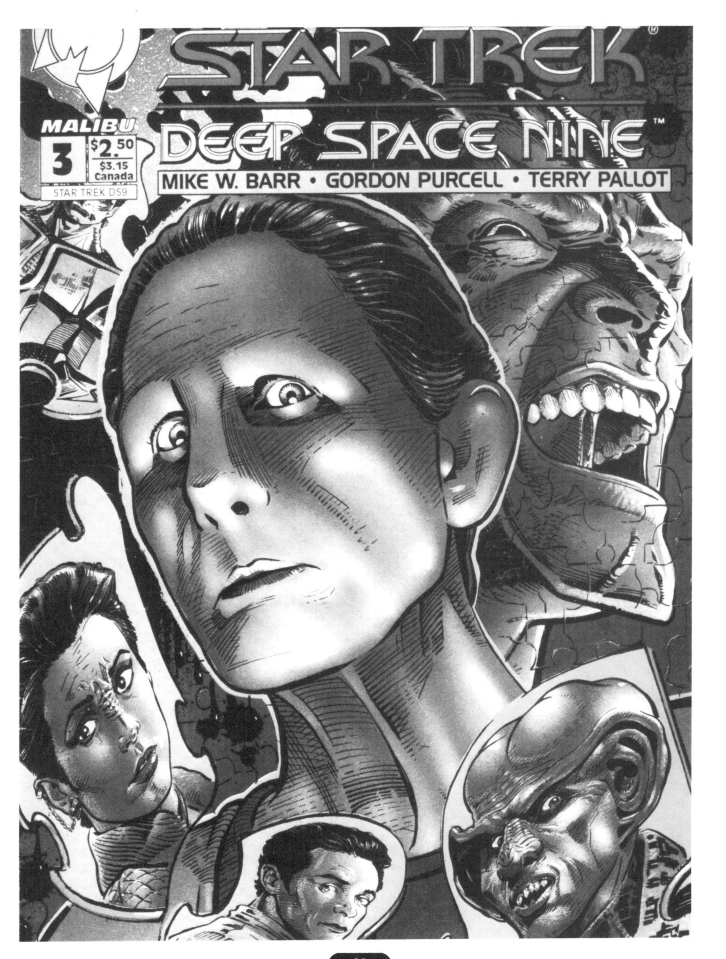

APPENDIX B

THE NEXT GENERATION ON DEEP SPACE

No one knows what it's like to produce a STAR TREK series better than those who work on one. Having toiled on their own side of the final frontier, the staff of THE NEXT GENERATION is just as opinionated about their sister series as the many fans who have raised their voices in praise — and in anger.

"The expectations were quite high from the pilot," said TNG Story Editor Rene Echevarria. "It was a feature, you could have shown it at the movies. They're coming out of the gate in much better shape than NEXT GENERATION did in terms of storytelling The discipline Michael brought to TNG he has carried on with DEEP SPACE NINE. I think Michael spent so much time working on the pilot that he really didn't have the time to put into those first three episodes, and they weren't as good as some of the later ones that have come. afterwards."

Naren Shankar worked on both series in the 1992/93 season as science advisor. "It's trying to find itself," he said of DEEP SPACE NINE's freshman year. "If you look at the first season of THE NEXT GENERATION, you barely recognize it today. I suspect that will be the case with DS9 a few years down the road. There's some very interesting areas to explore, both on the station and in the characters themselves. It will just be a matter of time before we find out what

those things are. In some ways, it makes me a little sad to see that the Enterprise is not going to be on television anymore because I was always a big fan of the idea that you kept going places. Here, it's different because you have to wait for things to come to you."

Story Editor Brannon Braga enthused, "I'm eager to write for DEEP SPACE NINE. It's very fascinating turf. I haven't really seen a lot of the episodes. I liked 'Dax.' 'Babel' on the other hand was one of the worst hours of television I've ever seen. It's a show that's just beginning and has had a better beginning than when this show started. What a great looking show as well. If I have one complaint about DEEP SPACE NINE so far, it's that they're still, in a way, trying to do NEXT GENERATION stories. I'd like to see more of the station and I'd like to see more of life on the station."

Offered veteran director Cliff Bole who has worked on THE NEXT GENERATION since its freshman year and who finally had his chance to board DEEP SPACE NINE when he directed the show's "Dramatis Personae" episode late first season, "Everybody is finding their character, but I compare that to the first season of STAR TREK. It's almost identical. I remember Brent was searching out his role. I think Sisko is still playing with some things. Fortunately for me, I had a show where I didn't have to deal with Avery and his normal character. I had ups and downs with him, which was great because he could do something different and didn't have to stay in char-

acter for the whole piece. We had a marvelous scene with Armin, when Armin and Odo were together. It's kind of the way I remember Charles Laughton and Peter Ustinov when I was doing script work on SPARTACUS. The screen just lit up when they were working together and that's what happens with these two guys, they're marvelous."

Bole pointed out that the only major differences between directing the two shows are the sets. "They are marvelous new sets and that was great fun for me," he said. "In its sixth year, everybody on THE NEXT GENERATION is really in the groove. By contrast, DEEP SPACE NINE is a little darker show. The characters are a little more ominous and the sets are a bigger challenge. They're tough to shoot. So, from a directing standpoint, that's basically the difference."

Ron Moore, who is the STAR TREK expert on staff, being well-versed in the original as well as THE NEXT GENERATION, commented, "I think it's off to a real good start. They're certainly off to a stronger start than we were. First season is a tough one. I thought the pilot was very well done. When I've been watching, I haven't really been watching it in terms of writing for it. It's been instructive to me in a different way of life. When you don't know what the text scene is supposed to be about, you try to follow it and sometimes when you hear the technobabble, you realize how you should write simpler because you don't know what they're saying."

No one is more finely

attuned to the early criticism that greeted DEEP SPACE NINE's launch than those on the NEXT GENERATION staff. The familiar refrain that characterized early letter writing campaigns that begged "pay attention to the show that matters", draws smiles from the NEXT GENERATION staff who perhaps feel a twinge of jealousy when they consider the financial and production resources that were marshaled to bring DEEP SPACE to the air. Said TNG Executive Producer Jeri Taylor, "We were feeling very much like second cousins at the beginning of the year because they had all of these fabulous aliens appearing on DEEP SPACE NINE. They just have hordes of them and if we wanted an alien, they'd have two pits in their forehead, like 'Aquiel.' Maybe a lot of time was going into developing the DEEP SPACE NINE people, but lately we've gotten wonderful people. The Uridian was one and there was a trader in 'Face of the Enemy.'"

"The money's being spent across the street," said Jonathan Frakes, who didn't have an opportunity to shoot on location for one of the episodes he directed of the NEXT GENERATION this season because of budgetary restrictions. "I don't think its a secret."

That feeling is typical among many of the NEXT GENERATION cast and crew when it is, in fact, arguable as to whether DEEP SPACE NINE

has had any impact — creative or financial — on THE NEXT GENERATION. Some feel that TREK's jump to the big screen may be to buoy the fortunes of its sister series. "I don't know how good that would be for DEEP SPACE NINE to have us continuing on television if they really want to launch them," said Marina Sirtis. "I've seen a few of episodes of DEEP SPACE, they have a different chemistry and it's a different atmosphere and dynamic they have going on over there. I look back on our first season and we've come a long way. I imagine they will grow as we grew. They're still finding their feet over there a little bit."

"I like it, though," said actor/director Frakes. "I wish we could see more of the sets. I think they're awesome. I feel like a lot of the show is being shot in close up and we're not getting the full value of the corridors. We see a lot of Quark's bar. Their bridge is fabulous, but — at least the way its cut — you don't see as much of those sets as when you go over and visit them. I'm dying to do one and I've made my pitch."

Frakes isn't the only director lobbying for a shot at directing DEEP SPACE NINE. Adam Nimoy, who made his directorial debut on sixth season STAR TREK: THE NEXT GENERATION, would love to find himself aboard Deep Space.

"There is a lot of charm to this new offshoot that is attractive to everybody," said Nimoy. "The characters, the sets, the stories. I'd love to be there. The point is that STAR TREK has become like a home to me. I know these people so well, and they're such good people, and they're so talented, from pre- to post-production, all the way down the line, this is a really good group of people. It's a winning team and I feel so privileged to be a part of it."

In evaluating DEEP SPACE NINE's maiden year, Jeri Taylor is upbeat about her bosses' new series. "I think DS9 is terrific. I think they are beginning to hit their stride now and Michael has done a magnificent job of finding the series in a very short time. I think there have been some hits and there have been some misses. That's got to happen, but it has very exciting potential, the public doesn't know those people as intimately as they know our people. There's six year of history, they care. DEEP SPACE NINE is still in a dancing around dating relationship and they need to get onto necking and heavy petting, and I'm sure they will."

APPENDIX C

A DAY IN THE LIFE:

ON THE SET WITH THE WILD & WACKY CAST OF DEEP SPACE NINE

By Mark A. Altman

(Reprinted from CINEFAN-TASTIQUE MAGAZINE in its original unabridged and unedited form by permission of the author)

Although the Paramount Pictures studio lot is replete with signs warning that photography is not allowed and no smoking or eating is permitted on the soundstages, one sign that is curiously absent is the road sign informing visitors that they are about to depart the 20th century and enter the 24th. Because, in fact, as you turn the corner by the Dressing Room building on the eastside of the Paramount lot, you will no longer feel as though you're in downtown Los Angeles on one of the dingier grottos of Melrose Avenue, but rather in the center of the STAR TREK universe.

Spanning six soundstages, the sprawling cement buildings are home to the sets of STAR TREK: THE NEXT GENERATION and across from them are the soundstages on which the DEEP SPACE NINE saga unfolds. "It's pretty bizarre," admitted Supervising Producer David Livingston. "There are six soundstages dedicated to two television shows and it can get pretty

heady at times. One night both shows were working and it was bizarre to look at all these people doing this science-fiction stuff."

Livingston, now literally wearing his director's hat — a Mickey Mouse baseball cap — holds his hands up, framing the shot, a moment in ops from the season ender, "In The Hands of The Prophets." He turns to me as I arrive on the set and hurls his headwear at me, "Remember Odd Job?" he quips. Clearly, the frivolity of the NEXT GENERATION set has permeated the air over at DEEP SPACE NINE, "Yeah," I reply, "And Harold Sakata was a little shorter than you." He nods approvingly. "That's my other beat," I note referring to the temporarily sidelined 007 saga.

Nana Visitor stands by the ops console in a black T-shirt during rehearsals, while Avery Brooks consults a script as Colm Meaney stands above at his station. So many directors who have worked on the show have failed to capture the grandiose vastness of the set along with the many subtle touches dotting every panel and console on its mutli-levels set. Equally impressive are the detailed graphics which can only be glimpsed fleetingly on screen, but can be seen along with the precise details delineated in each mini-visual.

Livingston, who Rick Berman calls the best director working on the show, calls action for the rehearsal and Avery descends the stairs. "Is it my imagination, or are we a little short handed today?" queries Brooks as Commander Benjamin Sisko.

Livingston rushes up,

hands flailing wildly in the air as Director of Photography Marvin Rush stands by him in jeans, formulating the dolly shot in their minds. "I think I'm giving you all the support I can," shoots back Nana in her guise of Major Kira. "It's not enough," Avery stammers before breaking into a hearty laugh. Siddig El Fadil and Rene Auberjonois enter from the turbo-lift and Livingston tells them to stand closer together. Siddig strides in saying, "I've managed to record DNA..." blowing the technobabble. Colm interjects the non-sequitur, "Phaser." "No," says Livingston. "That's the other shot. I think we have this one." Right.

Noted Colm Meaney later, "Technobabble is never easy. You're learning something that in a way doesn't make any sense. It's one of the chores of the job." Adds Siddig El Fadil, "I learned a trick. I try and learn it the day *before* now. That helps."

Nana starts doing jumping jacks on the set, apparently preparing for a Bajoran weight loss video as the camera dolly is brought out and the grips begin laying down wooden planks over the crevices in the metal floor for the dolly wheels to glide smoothly over. It's a much more difficult set to shoot than the bridge, with its smooth flooring and streamlined surfaces. As I'm watching, one of the extras approaches me. "You must be from CINEFANTASTIQUE," he shouts. "Why do you say that?" I reply. "You're taking notes — and everyone seems to know you," he answers. Can't argue with that.

His name is Kevin Grevioux, he's playing a security guard — although the actor harbors the secret hope of one day playing a Klingon or even a Cardassian. "I guess it's because I'm so tall," he says as one of the few people on the stage I actually have to look up to. He's been defending Deep Space Nine for nine months. Before joining Starfleet, the actor was studying to be a genetic engineer at Howard University, but had long ago been bitten by the sci-fi bug. By the time he contemplated graduate school, he was already in the throes of a radical career departure. Studying film and television in grad school after moving to L.A., Eddie Murphy spotted the would-be actor coming out of an elevator and gave him a role in one of his music videos, which was his first brush with the small screen. That's Hollywood. Needless to say, Kevin's a Trekkie, so duty on DEEP SPACE NINE rates as a good gig.

As the crew goes through the arduous and time-consuming process of re-lighting ops for the next shot, I proceed through the sets to refamiliarize myself with Deep Space Nine's phenomenal Herman Zimmerman-designed labyrinth of corridors and quarters. In one of the rooms, unused at present, stands a large cardboard standee of Captain Kirk brandishing a phaser. It's probably the first, and last time, you'll see Kirk aboard the station. In an adjoining room of the station, the chairs are set up for the cast as several extras lounge around, reading the paper.

Newspapers and magazines scatter the floor of the large room while several of the supernumeries converse among themselves.

As I head back to the bridge, er, ops, I pass a wild wall from the set, a panel built to be removed in order to accommodate certain camera angles which can be moved back easily when the camera is shooting another part of the large set. On it, the wild wall is marked "Oops 1."

Although I'm used to grabbing the cast on the fly, either in their trailers or outside the soundstage, this time I'm given my own office aboard Deep Space Nine. I'm moving up in the universe. Next to ops is a large room, I think it's Sisko's quarters, but I assume he won't mind me commandeering his living room for a few minutes while I interrogate the crew about their first year in space.

Much to my chagrin as a CINEFANTASTIQUE correspondent, I can't penetrate the harmonious veil that is given off by the ensemble because, like their counterparts across the street, or galaxy depending on how vivid your imagination is, they get along great. "I only think of the show as an ensemble piece," said Armin Shimerman. "You'll have to ask Mr. Brooks if he thinks differently because he does have that billing, but we think of it as an ensemble. We think of it as eight actors who will feature sometimes in an episode or not feature each week, just as you would in a rep company."

The difference is that a rep company makes Screen Actor's Guild scale and usually

performs in basements in dingy theaters in Manhattan. In this case, Shimerman's rep company is located in a "basement" that costs more than most Broadway shows. Said John DeLancie, best known as Q, of beaming aboard Deep Space Nine, "It wasn't any different than working on NEXT GENERATION. There were new people and it was nice to meet them. The days were long and it was very impressive, certainly the set and all that is much more impressive in a way, but in terms of just doing the work it was the same work and you hope you're going to find someone who, when you do a scene with them, push so that you can push back. That's what creates a scene."

Agreed Colm Meaney, who was on sabbatical for several weeks during the season to shoot Stephen Frears' new film, SNAPPER, "That kind of wonderful chemistry has carried over and the producers have to take a lot of credit for it. They've cast people with predominantly theater backgrounds, which has always been helpful on this show and this kind of work. I think that's been the major factor. Plus, they're good people."

Looking back at his first season off the Enterprise, Meaney smiles, "I think it's been a wonderful season. The fact that I was away in the middle of it broke it up into two halves. It doesn't feel as though it's been very long. Time flies when you're having fun and in terms of the success of the show, it's certainly been smoother and easier than I ever thought it would be.

We've got a great bunch of people. It's all good news, it's been a great nine months."

Nana Visitor thinks that the family feeling which characterizes life on and off the set can be found on the screen as well in Deep Space's later episodes. "There's nothing to replace that," says the actress of the on-screen chemistry between the cast-members. "You can get two great actors together and throw them together and the work will be good, but it won't be like people who have spent hours and hours everyday together and seen each other in every kind of mood; upset with personal stuff going on. There's just a deep understanding and chemistry and interest. When they say two actors have chemistry together, I think what they're saying is they're really interested in what the other one is saying off-camera, and on, and there's a respect and time given as opposed to saying this isn't my close-up. It might be my close-up but what are you saying to me — I think that's what chemistry is to me."

Co-Producer Peter Allan Fields laughs recalling how he's gone down to the set several times to introduce himself to a very focused Nana Visitor who doesn't ever seem to remember who he is. "I did write three shows for Kira and I kept going down to the set and introducing myself," he says. "I must have introduced myself 15 times. Every time I did a show that featured her that I thought was okay, I got a very polite how do you do — and I've given up. I'll probably walk up to Nana at the wrap party with a drink and

she'll take the drink and say thank you."

"I think 'If Wishes Were Horses' was the first time it all sort of gelled with Sid and my relationship," said Terry Farrell of Bashir's frustrated yearning to have his way with the voluptuous Trill science officer. "It took a long time before it all came together. I don't think it looked that way to anybody else, but I think this was the first time we as a cast were all really together and it all seemed to gell. It was an interesting moment where we realized we're like this basketball team that had found our camaraderie and felt comfortable."

Said El Fadil of the satisfaction of his character's desires when the comely Trill comes onto the good doctor, "I had no idea where to put myself, both me and the character. Having someone nibbling your ear while you're doing a scene is something I've never actually had to do. It's funny, because in that episode, I got what I wanted and didn't know what to do with it — partly because there was the real Dax floating around as well. It became a sort of split loyalty thing. I'd like to see more of that sort of stuff, please."

"'Move Along Home' was one of my favorites, but I really liked 'If Wishes Were Horses,'" says Terry Farrell. "We were all in both of them. I think that's why I liked 'If Wishes Were Horses'...besides kissing Siddig. That was very painless — and he pushed me off the bed. He made me feel so good and said 'I'm so sorry, you're just throwing me off.'"

Aboard a dark and

dreary space station, the best way to have fun is to keep the proceedings light and no one has mastered that fine art better than Terry Farrell. In "Babel," in which the crew becomes infected with an aphasia-like virus, she lay in a bed next to O'Brien. "That was great," she recalls. "Colm and I were pretending we were sicker in the infirmary than we were and were sticking paper up our nose so the challenge was to see that neither of us were going to be giggling by the time the camera reached us. It's sort of an infantile kind of humor."

The freshness of the new group of officers isn't lost on the directors who relish working with a new ensemble of cattle, er, actors as well as new sets. Director Winrich Kolbe worked with Avery Brooks on SPENSER FOR HIRE and now as Sisko For Hire. "It's obvious he is not Hawk anymore," says Kolbe. "He has mellowed and when he was Hawk *he was Hawk*. He just totally immersed himself into that character. I find that I see him a lot more relaxed, even though he still comes off as rather serious on DEEP SPACE NINE. But I think that's changing as well."

Adds Director Paul Lynch, who is directing Brooks again this summer in a new SPENSER: FOR HIRE telefilm, "On SPENSER he was one character and then he became much more mystical in his own series, A MAN CALLED HAWK. He's since gone onto DEEP SPACE where some of those elements definitely still exist, and now he's coming back to Hawk — so it will be a new

Hawk with all the elements of the original Hawk but developed more. There was a big, big audience of mostly college kids for Hawk because of the mystic powers. He was kind of like the David Carradine character in KUNG FU, a man of mysticism and vision in his own series, but now since the series went off the air I would think he'll bring that to bear on the new Hawk character. I think it's important that mystic element be present since he'll bring the DEEP SPACE audience — and if he takes Hawk into that mystic area, they're going to stay with him."

Lynch feels that Brooks truly discovered the character of Sisko mid-way through the season, "I was there at the beginning and he was sensational, but in 'Battle Lines' he really got it just soared. He's a wonderful actor, but he was just slowly feeling the character."

Said John DeLancie of his verbal and physical jousts with the new man who would be captain. "We were just starting. Patrick and I have developed a complicated relationship over six shows and it takes time to do that. It's not something you just kind of plop in. Avery and I will have to develop that complicated relationship. It's always dependent on what the script dictates. You need to have the material to do it with."

Over the course of shooting eighteen episodes and the pilot, not everything was a bed of roses. Terry Farrell remembers the middle of flu season where the sickness took its toll on the cast and crew far worse than the virus in "Babel." "Everybody

got sick," she recalls. "We all threw up the same weekend. The entire lot of Paramount; DEEP SPACE NINE, THE UNTOUCHABLES, everybody got the flu. That was the episode right before Christmas so we all felt like trapped animals, but it was great because we were all trapped together."

It must have helped your performance, I point out noting they were shooting "Move Along Home," an episode in which the cast was supposed to be discombobulated. "Obviously, you weren't here," she shoots back.

By the time, I've gotten Terry back in my office, she's shot her last scene which was greeted by a rousing chorus of cheers followed by a receiving line of kisses and hugs that greeted the actress after finishing her final scene of the season. Now, it's time to think about next year. "What if I don't come back? Remember Gates?" she says. I tell her she's more neurotic than Jason Alexander on SEINFELD, which seems to calm her down for a minute...but only a minute. "You'll be back," I assure her. "God, I hope so" she says in a moment of rare serious contemplation. "I love doing this show."

"I'd like to explore different lifetimes that I've had," she ponders about next season. "Not just Curson, other facets of the seven lifetimes that I've had. I'd like to go to the planet where I'm from. I like how my relationship has developed with Nana, even though its been small. We've had some things together this year. In the beginning, we had nothing. One time I said something sar-

castic to her about how someone on the station could use my meditation technique and Kira kind of had a laugh and I said, 'Yeah, so could you' but they cut it out of the show because I think it looked a little too catty."

El Fadil considers his hopes for the second year of the show as Yes and John Lennon play on the stereo in the background in his trailer. "There's no rush for him to become a wise old man," the actor speculates. "I'd like for him to learn some more about other types of medicine, alternative medicine, which must still be around in the 24th century because as a young man he can become enthusiastic about that without having to change too much. Maybe, some semblance of the flirty side can get bigger and knowing that these people bite back. I'd like him to know that as opposed to just completely getting laid out with a left hook anytime he goes near any woman."

Adds the Sudanese actor, "It's fun and rip roaring and if he gets a chance to be a little philosophical about something one day, that would be nice too. But I can't ask to play every character on the show all in one. I've got to let other characters do their thing too."

After a long day in DEEP SPACE, I pack up to leave. As I take one last long lingering look at ops, Terry Farrell yells out, "I hope I didn't harass you too much." Grinning as I leave the 24th century, I answer, "You can harass me anytime."

APPENDIX D

QUESTION & ANSWER SESSION

STAR TREK: DEEP SPACE NINE

January 13, 1993

THOSE PRESENT:

Rick Berman, Michael Piller, Avery Brooks, Rene Auberjonois, Siddig El Fadil, Terry Farrell, Cirroc Lofton, Colm Meaney, Armin Shimerman, Nana Visitor

Q: Quark seems like a much more upscale Ferengi than what we're used to. Was there an intent to make him more of a successful and accomplished Ferengi than some of the ones you've seen in the past?

ARMIN SHIMERMAN: I think that's more an answer for our writers than for me. But, I hope so. I also think that you get to know Quark a lot better than you ever got to know any Ferengi before, and as you get to know him more he will of course have more and more depth.

Q: The core fans of STAR TREK are an important part of the success of the show. Did you go to them to get a consensus first of what they might like and what they might not like?

RICK BERMAN: I think we're always going to them in a sense, because there is the interaction between the producers and the fans. On STAR TREK I think it's different than on most other television shows because of all the letters and the various magazines and fan clubs. So we're constantly in touch with at least the more verbal members of our fans and we certainly got a feeling from them that they were more than willing to embrace another STAR TREK series.

Q: Mr. Meaney, would you discuss your part in the series as far as being the voyage between GENERATION and DEEP SPACE? Did you personally say, "I want more time," or did they come to you and say, "We want one character who will bring fans over..."?

COLM MEANEY: I think they were looking for a way to get me off the Enterprise. Correct me if I'm wrong here, guys. There was more written for me on NEXT GENERATION, but obviously with the set cast over there, there was only so much room for the development of every character, and when this opportunity came up....

RICK BERMAN: We needed a token Irishman on the show.

COLM MEANEY: Obviously it is in one sense a bridge between the Enterprise. But the fact that the show has happened shows that there is obviously room for movement between the show and, obviously it is....yes, I am a connection with the Enterprise.

Q: I want to address the resurgence of science fiction on television. This program audience is the leading example of that. But there are a lot of other things going on. Why is science fiction so big all of a sudden? And also, a few words about the enduring appeal of it, going back to Jules Verne. Sometimes it's quiescent and then it comes back again. It never entirely goes away.

ARMIN SHIMERMAN: I think part of that is just the child in all the adults. It appeals to that, and when you also add in wonderful science fiction where you tease the mind as well, the people are going to come in flocks. I'm sure there are other ideas as well.

RICK BERMAN: I think, without feeling too good about ourselves, one of the reasons for the resurgence going on right now in science fiction is

Armin Shimerman, sans Ferengi make-up, meets with his fans at a "Star Trek" convention (photo copyright ©1994 Karen Witkowski)

people trying to accomplish what THE NEXT GENERATION accomplished over the last five years, which is a successful one-hour television series.

Q: Mr. Brooks, I remember there was a long delay in casting of the lead role, and everybody realized that was the important role, and so forth. What was your first reaction to it, and what process did you have to go through to decide you wanted to do it?

AVERY BROOKS: Actually it happened very quickly for me. I came somewhere near the end of the delay, so I didn't have time to think about it. It all happened very, very fast. I was in the Caribbean actually, and I talked to my agent and he asked me if I was a fan of STAR TREK. I said, "Well, I watch it of course." He said I have a script you might want to read. I read it and was thrilled about it, actually. The writing was extraordinary, the story very compelling. And so I pursued it. And then — this is actually true — I was on my way to lay down something on tape in New York, and my car started to slip out of gear. So I called my wife and said I don't know if I can make it, and so I called the people frantically and said I don't think I can make it in. But actually they let me do it again, and then I was

out of town again. They said, "We need you to come to California now." I said, "I'm in Atlanta." So then I flew out here and it all happened very, very fast, and I'm thrilled.

Q: What quality were you looking for in the casting of Sisko?

MICHAEL PILLER: I think you can see the quality just sitting here today. You walk into the room at the end of that journey, and we knew we had found our Sisko. We had been looking for a quality that continued with the heroic leadership potential, but we knew that very big boots had to be filled. We had two great stars in the leadership role of captains and commanders in the past, and it was very difficult to find someone who really impressed everybody in the room with the presence of command that Avery did.

RICK BERMAN: I think the key is the word "presence". We needed someone who could match or hopefully exceed the sense of presence that Patrick Stewart I think exudes on a pretty regular basis as Captain Picard. We didn't want to go backwards, we wanted to go forwards in that, and that's what we were looking for. We were looking for a good actor, but more than anything we

were looking for someone with that sense of commanding presence which this guy seems to give us.

Q: Just to follow that real quickly, Mr. Brooks, did you see in the new STAR TREK a sort of frenzy that the fans of the show tend to have?

AVERY BROOKS: After we shot the pilot, even walking down the streets of the Paramount lot, people who have never spoken to me before suddenly say, "Oh, hello, how are you?" So that's very different. I of course have been aware of the phenomenon of STAR TREK. I grew up here, so that if I thought about it, I mean the size of it, I suppose that I would find it difficult to come to work. But I'm very, very glad, and I'm very curious, you know, to be involved in something this size.

Q: Are you worried about typecasting?

AVERY BROOKS: The fact of the matter is that I have been blessed with a thunderbolt artistically before this moment. I've done a myriad of things. I mean, for example, I've been doing Paul Robeson for a decade. Those kinds of things I hope I'll be able to continue to do to separate myself from the Sisko character, even though of course people will say, "Yeah, that's Benjamin Sisko." But I hope as an artist that also I'll be able to — as we all hope — do anything. So sometimes I'm Sisko and sometimes I'm not.

Q: To the producers. You have taken the new STAR TREK on a rather grittier journey. The ship itself is not as tidy even as we stepped out of the Enterprise. The plots are a lot deeper, darker. I realize you've only been on a couple of weeks, but have you heard from anyone about this, not a veering of direction, but a subtle shifting of gears here? I have one other question. Gene Roddenberry was always noted for saying that, "It's not STAR TREK unless I say it's STAR TREK." I realize he's no longer with us, but do you think that if he was alive he would say, "I say this is STAR TREK."?

RICK BERMAN: I think we were both very close to Gene, and I think Gene learned quite early in THE NEXT GENERATION process that we could be trusted with STAR TREK. I came in and had to learn a whole new language, not just the language of the future but the language of Gene Roddenberry's future, which is a very specific posi-

tive vision of man's potential in the future. When we developed this new series, literally every step of the way we had Gene sitting on our shoulders. And many things were rejected because "Gene wouldn't buy that." And I very much believe, and Michael does as well, that Gene would be very pleased with the way this has gone. I do think that we are not producing a show that's quite as dark as a lot of the press have made it out to be. That's a little bit inaccurate. We've developed a little bit more conflict than existed in STAR TREK, and we did that quite purposely, when we put our characters on a space station that's to some degree inhospitable to them as opposed to the very comfortable USS Enterprise, but that was all done for a very specific purpose to be able to build in a little bit more conflict that we felt we lacked to some degree with THE NEXT GENERATION.

MICHAEL PILLER: It's conflict on every level we could find it. They are in conflict with their environment, as has already been said. They are in conflict with each other because the Enterprise had had everybody with the same agenda. Everybody was basically on a mission and they all got along very well. Here, they're thrown

together with aliens, different species. All have to coexist together on the same space station. All of them have different agendas and different goals. Quark over there wants to fill his pockets, and Odo wants to catch him. Right there you have conflict. We have Major Kira as our Bajoran liaison and here again is a very deliberate tilt. We made the Bajorans a very mystical, spiritual people, as different from the humanist, logical humans of the 24th century as we could. So, while we protect the vision of humanity that we inherit from Gene, we put that in direct conflict with a very different kind of people. So those people are in conflict on every level.

RICK BERMAN: I just want to add one thing. Gene Roddenberry was a great believer in not wanting any conflict between the characters on the Enterprise, which was very frustrating for us because that's what good drama is borne from. And we didn't want to break Gene's rules, and in so doing there still is not a lot of conflict between Starfleet officers, that we have developed the concept of the environment and we put our people into an environment where there are a lot of characters who are not Starfleet officers that enable us

Rene Auberjonois and Odo's bed (photo copyright ©1994 Karen Witkowski)

to develop that conflict.

MICHAEL PILLER: And Gene also believed a great deal in the diversity of species and that there was room for all these different species in the universe. We have just not made them regularly a part of the show.

Q: I have a question for Rene Auberjonois. Have you studied Spock or Data? How did you prepare for your character?

RENE AUBERJONOIS: No, I haven't studied Spock or Data any more than anybody in an audience watching the show does. I think there are certain similarities, but I think the differences are more striking. The thing about Odo that I find fascinating is that there is a kind pain in him because he is forced to take on a humanoid shape, which is unlike those other characters that you mentioned. He is in a position where he is observing humanity but he is not wishing he were human. He wishes he could find out exactly who he is and where he comes from, and if there are any others like him in existence. So, in answer to your question, no I haven't studied Spock or Data. I'm very much involved with trying to figure out who Odo is.

Q: I have a question for Ms. Visitor. I can't remember a more forceful female character in either of the first two STAR TREK series, and I realize I've just seen the first episode, but certainly your character is rather quick to establish a presence, and a forceful one on the show. Is this the way you saw the character? Is this the way it was on the page, or is it a combination of both?

NANA VISITOR: This is the way it was on the page. That was one reason I was so excited when I received the script and read a woman who was a powerful woman — she was

THE DEEP SPACE LOGBOOK

first officer, so she was in command, but she wasn't just politically correct, because she's not perfect. She doesn't do everything just right and always knows the right thing to think and do. She makes mistakes, she's not sure within herself. And so, the fact that she is a woman suddenly wasn't an issue anymore. It was a species who had spirituality, who had aggressiveness, who had ideas of her own. We just skipped that in a sense, and she's a truthful, emotional being, and that was very exciting, and it was a matter of me filling out the spaces of the character.

Q: A little question for the Sisko kid. Can you tell us a little bit about what it's like joining this bunch, and are you a big STAR TREK fan, and do your friends envy you?

CIRROC LOFTON: I watch STAR TREK occasionally. I'm not a Trekkie, but I do watch the show. My friends, they see me in a different light because I'm on the show. We don't do different things, but they talk to me differently and they see me as Jake and not Cirroc anymore. It's kind of a mix. But I enjoy being Jake Sisko.

Q: For the creators, could you talk about the morphing process for the

Odo character?

RICK BERMAN: Morphing covers a lot of territory. Basically a computerized process is going from one image to another. We are using a version of that and obviously we are doing our best to try to not make it exactly the same as people got used to in things like TERMINATOR and certain television commercials, but we are using it and we're doing it within our budget, and we don't do it in every episode, and we're fine-tuning it in each episode. It's getting a little bit more different and we hope a little better as we go along.

RENE AUBERJONOIS: Personally, I like the fact that it's not in every episode because I think that who Odo is is the deep question to the answer, and so I'm really thrilled about that. I never know what it's going to look like until I see it on the screen. Last night I saw the first one-hour episode where I'm a rat and then I become myself again. The day they shot the rat's work I didn't work, obviously. I came in the next day and everybody was saying, "Hey, you were great yesterday. It's wonderful what you did." And I was. It was wonderful to see it last night. I just sit there and go, "Whooh!" It's incredible.

Q: Actors and actresses are called on to play a wide variety of roles, but there probably aren't too many young women who are asked to play 300-year-old men. What do you do to prepare yourself for that kind of part? What do you think about to get into that role?

TERRY FARRELL: This took me a lifetime to get. I don't know how to explain it. I think it's a maternal thing, honestly, because being 328, she's obviously older than anybody else. So I guess I look at it this way. If I was to protect anyone, it would be like protecting my niece. I've lived more than she has, and if I was going to protect anyone I would want to die first to let them all live, because I've already lived so many lifetimes. I've seen so much that it would seem unfair to not put them first. I guess that's what I take with me when I think about those things.

Q: Mr. Berman. With a male commander and female first officer, was this an attempt to go back to what Mr. Roddenberry was originally thinking when he did the first STAR TREK pilot?

RICK BERMAN: You have two ways of going — one is a male

Dr. Julian Bashir in his civvies, a.k.a. Siddig El Fadil at a convention (photo copyright ©1994 Karen Witkowski)

and one is a female and it just seemed like the right thing to do. I don't think we did it to be politically correct. I don't think we did it to mimic the original STAR TREK. We did it because it felt right as we were creating the characters.

Q: Did you ever consider having a woman in charge?

RICK BERMAN: Yes we did. We also finally decided not to, but that was certainly the role of Sisko. It was definitely discussed that Sisko might be a woman.

Q: Rick, I'm a little confused. You said earlier that you were a little concerned about critics who called the show dark, yet you put those conflicts in every time and you want to build conflict so you have the drama.

RICK BERMAN: I think dark to me as the connotation of the show having a bleak or an eerie quality to it, which I don't believe it will. Our series is going to have the same uplifting messages, we hope, and deal with the same metaphorical way of approaching the future that both of Gene Roddenberry's series did previously. I don't think it's going to be "dark" in

terms of a dark outlook toward the future, and that's where I think it was misunderstood.

I got a letter from like 25 grade school children in the middle of the country, saying "We've read" — this was before the show premiered — "We've read this is going to be a dark new series," and, with their teachers' help, they were saying, "Please don't do this, we use this as a tool of hope, of teaching potential, and so forth. Don't change the vision." That's what scares us when the misinterpretation is put to the word "darkness." See, in conflict there's also humor. That's the secret of all situation comedies, that you have an enduring conflict. In our case, we have found, and I think you'll see as the show continues, that the kind of conflict here also yields a certain kind of humor within the context of our kind of drama.

I think there's a lot more humor in this show than there is in THE NEXT GENERATION, certainly in the first 10 episodes that we have been involved with so far.

Q: Rick and Michael, was the first episode exactly as you envisioned it?

RICK BERMAN: Yes. This is a very collective process, making a two-hour film, or making any kind of television program

or film, and it evolves slowly. One thing, just to contradict Nana down there a little bit. She asked if she had anything to do with creating this character, or whether it was on the page, and she said it was on the page. I don't believe that's really true, I think we create characters and then we hire actors to play those characters and the actors bring in many instances as much to those characters as we did in creating them, and it's that marriage that ends up becoming either a character that works or doesn't. And I think the same thing is true with every other element of the show. It's something that you've got to be very open about and watch evolve, as we have over the last year.

MICHAEL PILLER: I think it's got to be said, though, that — I can't think of anywhere else in town, and this is going to sound like I'm kissing up here, but I can't imagine anywhere else in town where the vision that we started with could be executed without the financial and creative support that this studio gave, and it's directly the result of the first-run syndicated business and the decision to finance this at the full freight.

Q: Mr. Brooks has already answered this question, but the other actors....did you come into this thinking that 30 years from now you could be walking down the street and people would be recognizing you from what you're doing now? Is it something that comes into your consciousness?

ARMIN SHIMERMAN: I don't have that problem.

NANA VISITOR: No, actually. The process was getting this wonderful job and doing it, and some of the days were 16 hours — long days — and being totally immersed in that, and you're in this operational center, you're in this world, and people come up to you and say, "Do you know what this means?" Maybe there's some kind of safety valve that's keeping me from understanding it. But I don't. All I know is I'm doing this great part and it's probably something that maybe for the first time in my career I'm really proud of. I'm really proud of the quality. And what happens beyond that....I guess I'll see. But now, it hasn't computed for me at all.

Q: Siddig, were you influenced by any of the previous STAR TREK doctors?

SIDDIG EL FADIL: I don't think I do bring anything from the previous doctors. I just want to look as though I'm having fun, because that's

what I am, and I think that's infectious. So, I just try to play everything as it comes. It's a naive character for whom everything is a new experience and very fun.

Q: Is it a stigma being a syndicated show as opposed to a network show?

MICHAEL PILLER: I'll be very frank about the part where [it is]....the creative community. It is hard to be seen and recognized because a lot of the people think that the network game is still the game in town. Patrick Stewart, and certainly members who are sitting with me today, and other members of the cast of THE NEXT GENERATION, have not been nominated for wonderful performances, and the writers and directors of the show have not been nominated. We have been honored by the technical and creative arts side, where the community supports its own and knows the kind of work that we're doing. But, there is one last piece that is still remaining.

Q: Mr. Brooks, you look a lot less intense than at a previous press conference. Is this because of the role you're playing; are you more content or comfortable with the role?

AVERY BROOKS: Well, I suppose because I'm older, I'm better. But, yes, as I recall at that press conference there wasn't the same kind of warm feeling and congeniality. And so, I suppose, my posture more than anything was to defend myself and to defend the work. In this case, it is quite a different matter. If you recall, I mean just to hearken back, the first question was why? You see what I mean. Certainly now we're in an environment where nobody is asking why. Because this is a quarter century old. So, it's quite a different matter. The other thing that must be said, of course, and I tried to mention it a little bit earlier, but as an actor, just as a musician, that you hope you'll be able to do anything. I can go right back there. But, I'm going to be on vision of Sisko now. I was looking at this film a couple of months ago. It was an early sci-fi film and Walter Pidgeon was in it. He's an admiral. He turned to this character and he said, "All it takes for a strong commander is to have a strong voice and no brains." And I said to myself, "Well, I qualify for one of the two."

Q: I have a question for the producers. What are some of the things that you would like to say about our world by dealing with the fanta-

Nana Visitor does the convention circuit to help promote "DS9" and to meet with her fans (photo copyright ©1994 Karen Witkowski)

sy world that you write about?

MICHAEL PILLER: That's a long question, and the only thing I can sort of do to answer it is to say that every time we go to the writers' board and try to break a story, we try to find out what is our show about and how we explore the human condition, and one of your colleagues in NEWSWEEK followed that comment with an, "Oh please," like it's a violation of science fiction genre to do these characterizations and to have high goals, but that's a rap we're willing to take. In the coming episodes we deal with the futility of war. We deal with the morality of hunting. We deal with racism. What else comes to mind?

RICK BERMAN: You know, I think what science fiction has always done and what STAR TREK has always done is enable us to metaphorically deal with virtually any subject. We attempt to deal with contemporary subjects, but subjects slightly differently, as science fiction allows us to do, and to have people look at them and hopefully to provoke some thought in a unique way. We've done that for the last five and a half years on THE NEXT GENERATION and we intend to keep doing it with this show.

Q: Will there be much crossover between the shows?

MICHAEL PILLER: I think it's terribly important that this series establish itself and establish itself on its own merits. I think that's a decision that was made in the early stages of THE NEXT GENERATION, not to depend a lot on the guest stars and traditions from the original show. You will, however, see some members of the universe that was crated in THE NEXT GENERATION — visits by Q and Mrs. Troi and other subsidiary characters who have been known and loved. But, ultimately, we will be focusing on our characters, putting them in the middle of stories, and if a story naturally brings the Enterprise or a member of the Enterprise crew to the space station, we won't fight it. So we're not going out of our way to employ them to hype this show. In fact, the only other example of it is on THE NEXT GENERATION when we actually visit Deep Space Nine on that show, as opposed to going the other way and crossing over this way on this show.

Q: Is the appetite for STAR TREK finite? Are you hatching another series as we speak?

RICK BERMAN: I don't think there's any such thing as an endless wealth. I think that right now having two shows on the air seems to be something that our audience is willing to happily accept. We're ten episodes into a series that we hope is going to run a long time, and we're at this moment not thinking about an additional STAR TREK TV series.

Naturally, as has recently come to bear, Paramount is planning on launching its own network in January '95, cornerstoned by yet another series inspired by Gene Roddenberry's creation, STAR TREK: VOYAGER.

CAPTAIN'S LOGS

THE COMPLETE TREK VOYAGES

By
Edward Gross
&
Mark A. Altman

EXPLORING DEEP SPACE

AND BEYOND

By Mark A. Altman and David Ian Solter

B□XTREE